"Keith Carroll brilliantly shows the way to be Jesus on display in the 21st century without letting the culture around us squeeze us into its mold. Keith's practical directives allow the reader to grasp the way to thrive and not just survive this journey on planet earth!"

Jackie Kendall, best-selling author and national speaker

"Mentally stimulating and spiritually provoking, *The Christ Culture* is not only a joy to read, it is also a great reflection of the Lord's desire for us. Keith Carroll has found a way to lovingly, yet powerfully, provoke us to come into the true nature of 'Christ in us.' This is one of the most informative books in our day, a literary masterpiece on many levels."

Sandra Querin, JD, MBA, Thd.
Pastor, The Revival Center, Clovis, CA

"I have reviewed countless manuscripts over the past 30 years, but few have had this clarity and even fewer carried the dynamic truth of the Word with such simplicity."

Don Nori Sr., founder, Destiny Image Publishers

"There are a lot of 'oohs' and 'ahs' as the light turns on."

D. Erdmann, Wisconsin

"In the decade I have known Keith Carroll, his insights have never ceased to amaze me, while helping shape my own along the way. A conversation with him will keep you thinking for days. His insights are eye-opening. To have those thoughts captured on the written page is priceless. Keith has written a book you will refer to again and again and highly recommend to others. Read, think, study, share. Repeat. A rare combination indeed."

Catherine Zoller, author of The Rhyme and Reason Series

"I have never encountered any book quite as eloquently written as this one. Keith Carroll's teaching on God's ways is not only life changing but provides an entirely different way of thinking. I highly recommend this book to anyone looking for purpose and meaning in life. *The Christ Culture* is a roadmap that takes you on a remarkable journey that will leave you completely and utterly transformed."

Mary E. Banks, MSM, SPHR, President, WOW Consulting Group, author of Living by Faith 9 to 5

THE CHRIST CULTURE

A Way of Life Like No Other

Keith Carroll

PRESS

Newburg, Pennsylvania

ISBN 978-0-9860923-1-2 (print)
For Worldwide Distribution
Printed in the U.S.A.

Relate To God Press
PO Box 240
Newburg, PA 17240

Table of Contents

Special Thanks

*To the inspiring contribution of
my wife, Nancy; Thelma and Gary Diehl;
Delores Ocker; and Alice and Rocky Rockwell,
the Relate to God Ministry team*

*And to Sam and Daphne Eaton,
and Glen Reed for their deeply
rewarding fellowship*

Introduction

The Christ Culture is a fresh way of looking at God's desire for our life on the earth. The culture of Christ is an atmosphere where God's inspiring presence is experienced and Christ-like attitudes and behaviors are encouraged. Participants believe in God and are responsive to His inspirational input.

The culture of Christ is not limited to a religion or ethnic people, nor is it governed by any organization. It is much more than a belief system or religious activity. The culture of Christ is a nutrient rich environment where lives improve due to a receptive submission to our heavenly Father's guiding presence.

The Old Testament foretold of a time when God would establish His governing presence on the earth. Daniel said it would come after the successive historical reigns of Babylon, Medo-Persia, and Greece, during the fourth kingdom—the Roman Empire

> *In the days of those kings the God of heaven will set up a kingdom which will never be destroyed* (Daniel 2:44).

Isaiah also prophesied that when this time came, God would establish a governing presence (as a kingdom) that would continue to increase until His influencing presence filled the whole earth.

> *There will be no end to the increase of His government...to establish it...from then on and forevermore* (Isaiah 9:7).

Both writers declared this governing presence of God would endure and increase from then on, forevermore. When Jesus began His public ministry, He declared the prophesied time had come for God's kingdom influence. He introduced our heavenly Father's governing presence 2000 years ago while the Roman Empire ruled.

Jesus came…preaching the gospel [good news] *of God, and saying, "The time is fulfilled, and the kingdom of God is at hand; repent and believe in the gospel"* (Mark 1:14-15).

The Gospel of John proclaimed Jesus Christ is the expression of God that came to earth to demonstrate our heavenly Father's desire to dwell with us as the light of our life (see John 1:1-5, 9-14).

In the first book of the New Testament, Matthew identified Jesus as "Christ" (1:16) and as "Emmanuel" (1:23). When we consider that the word Christ means "anointed" and the name Emmanuel means "God with us," we are able to realize that Jesus was "The anointing presence of God that came to dwell among people."

The word "Christ" however, speaks of more than the historical Jesus. In Acts 4:26-27 Christ is used to speak of God's anointing on Jesus. Christ refers to the presence of God that comes into our midst to inspire, anoint, influence, lead, and guide us.

Jesus introduced the culture of Christ as the anointing presence of God that would influence lives from that time forward. God has continued to dwell among the willing. He seeks to lead and guide us through our times and seasons, generation after generation.

The culture of Christ is a lot like the atmospheric air. The movement of atmospheric air is all around us even though we don't always take notice. Its reality becomes obvious when its movement affects natural objects. Most everyone has sensed God's protective or inspiring presence at one time or another.

Jesus referred to the atmosphere of the culture of Christ when He spoke of people who are spiritually alive and relate to God in some manner. To the natural eye they are as indiscernible as the wind.

> *The wind blows where it wishes and you hear the sound of it, but do not know where it comes from and where it is going; so is everyone who is born of the Spirit* (John 3:8).

Jesus, as the presence of God among us, began changing lives then and has continued to influence life throughout human history. Today, as then, God's presence continues to inspire all who receive Him. Everybody is invited to experience this way of living.

The culture of Christ is "not of this world" because it is not located in any particular community or geographic area. However, the people of this culture function in this world without being ruled by its attitudes or way of life. While the natural eye cannot see the form of this culture, participants are discerned most anywhere. We are recognized by our Christ-like attitude, character and activity.

Our heavenly Father invites all of us into the fellowship of His presence. This is not a hope (as a delayed expectation) but is a living reality for life in this world. The people of this culture experience God as a presence that seems to always be near.

Preface

In *The Christ Culture* we describe an atmosphere on the earth where the inspiring presence of God is experienced. This is not a hope or delayed expectation but a reality for our life in this world.

As the earthly life of Jesus concluded, He said He would never leave nor forsake us, that He would always be with us (see Matthew 28:20; Hebrews 13:5-6). Believing this, we see that He intends to lead and guide followers, as God's governing presence among us.

We partake of the culture of Christ as we respond to God's inspiring presence. It began changing the world 2000 years ago and has continued to influence lives throughout history.

Anyone can partake of this culture anywhere in the world because it is not restricted to any natural location. Partaking of this culture can be strange at first. As we immerse ourselves into this way of living, eventually we prefer its ways over our previous norms.

Scripture identifies the "relational ways of God" as processes that He uses to help us grow to reflect and resemble His heart. The first three chapters of *The Christ Culture* enable us to more fully appreciate the heart and nature of God.

We realize: 1) **Life** is our process of becoming what God has created us to be; 2) **Salvation** is the process God uses to transform offspring into disciplined children; and 3) **Forgiveness** is God's open invitation for us to partake of the fellowship of His presence.

The next five chapters enable us to clearly see how the ways of God transforms us into the people He designed us to become. We recognize: 4) **Repentance** unleashes the benefits of God's forgiveness upon us; 5) **Changes** we go through teach us to be more adjustable; and 6) **Balance** is the perspective that the Prince of Peace brings into our life.

Additionally, we discover how our 7) **Interaction** with God and one another facilitates our maturing process; then we begin to see that our godly 8) **Forgiving** inspires others to partake of the fellowship of God's presence that dwells among us and in our midst.

In *The Christ Culture* we focus on the primary maturing activity that takes place as we experience the influencing presence of God and learn to follow His inspiring lead.

God's ways become a major influence over how we interact with each other. Instead of talking about religion, we encourage each other to be faithful to God and His ways. We learn to share what we sense God is saying and doing in our lives and in our communities instead of complaining about what others are doing.

God has always desired to dwell with His human children. He started in the Garden of Eden when He communed daily with Adam and Eve. Their turning aside to consider another way is what began humanity's separation from His guiding presence.

As a great Father, God wants to lead and guide us through our life experience. He provides His guiding influence in the culture of Christ. Our level of acceptance, individually and collectively, determines how abundant our life experience is.

The ways of God reveal a lot about our heavenly Father's character, attitude, and personality. As we learn more about God, we are better able to reflect and resemble His heart in the world around us. Our heavenly Father invites each of us into the fellowship of His presence. To what degree are we listening, observing, and following His lead?

Join with me on a journey of discovery to learn more about how to live as a thriving participant of the culture of Christ.

Chapter 1

The Way of Life Develops Us

There once was a water bearer who had the task of carrying water from a stream to his master's house over a mile away. He carried two jugs of water attached to either end of a pole, which he carried across his shoulders. One pot was perfect but the second one had a crack in its side.

Every day, the water bearer would carry the empty pots to the stream, fill them to the brim, and then carry them home. The cracked pot leaked water steadily as the bearer went on his way, so only half a pot of water was left in the cracked pot by the time the water bearer got to his master's house.

After a year of leaking water, the cracked pot finally spoke to the water bearer. "I am sorry for leaking water along the way. I have cut your productivity and am so ashamed I have not delivered the full amount of water I was designed to carry."

The water bearer replied, "Today when we go along the path, I want you to notice the beautiful flowers growing next to the path."

When they got home, the water bearer said to the cracked pot, "I knew you had a leak and I thought to take advantage of it. Several months ago I planted flower seeds along the path.

"The water you have leaked did not go to waste. It watered the flowers every day. Now they are beautiful and I have been able to pick them to decorate my master's table. Without your flaw, this would not have been possible."

Each of us has our own unique flaws. We're all cracked pots. But it's the cracks and flaws we have that make each of our lives so very interesting and rewarding.

We want to receive each person for who they are and look for the good in them. There is a lot of good out there. There is a lot of good in you!

What Is Life About?

It is said, "Life is a journey, not a destination." Scripture adds depth to this phrase by teaching us that we are birthed into life as God's offspring. We are intended to grow and develop as His children. Life is our earthly journey of development.

Humanity began in the heart of God as a desire for offspring who would grow and develop under His fatherly care. To facilitate the process of birthing and developing offspring, God created the natural realm. He made this natural realm and process for us!

And what a beautiful and diverse creation the natural realm is! Can you believe there are more than 18,000 butterfly species in the world? It gets even more amazing: There are about 1,250,000 identified species of animals. As a comparison, almost 300,000 plant species are known.

These numbers do not account for species that have not yet been captured or described scientifically. Scientists estimate there may be as many as 10-30 million unidentified insect species, many of them living in rainforests.

With all its ability, science is not able to create life, nor have scientists found it anywhere else in the universe. Life in this earth is unique from all of creation—it has the ability to reproduce! Life truly is amazing.

God created the material universe and He formed the earth to function with all its life forms and growth processes. He relates to these creations as their Creator. Humanity, however, is different: God relates to each of us as a parent. No other creatures out of all the millions in existence are referred to as His offspring.

Our heavenly Father started with just two humans, and today there are more than 7 billion living persons. That's a lot of kids! All of creation reflects something of God's glory, but we are uniquely made to manifest more of His personhood and nature. As offspring of God we are birthed into existence with a heavenly purpose.

Then God said, "Let Us make man in Our image, according to Our likeness" (Genesis 1:26).

God said He intends for each of us to grow and develop into His image and likeness. In the following pages we will clarify that offspring are birthed with the potential to become children who respond to the guidance of our heavenly Father, we progressively become what God has intended us to be.

When God said, "Let Us...in Our...according to Our likeness," He referred to the three primary visuals that He uses to relate to His earthly offspring. God reveals Himself to humanity as our Father, who creatively brings us into existence and then oversees our development.

> *For this reason I bow my knees before the Father, from whom every family in heaven and on earth derives its name* [identity] (Ephesians 3:14-15).

God also reveals Himself to mankind as His foremost Son, Jesus Christ, to demonstrate to everyone what we are designed to become. Jesus is the ideal child of God.

> *And the Word became flesh, and dwelt among us, and we saw His glory, glory as of the only begotten from the Father, full of grace and truth* (John 1:14).

Additionally, God reveals Himself to us as a Holy Spirit presence, so He can personally lead each of us through life's developmental experiences.

> *But when He, the Spirit of truth, comes, He will guide you into all the truth* (John 16:13).

The Genesis 1:26 verse that we have quoted has an additional insight we want to notice. The Hebrew word translated "image" is *tselem*, which means: an image that reflects the original, as a reflection or a shadow. We are designed to reflect God.

Additionally, the Hebrew word translated "likeness" is *demuwth*, which is a resemblance that possesses some, but not all, of the characteristics of the original. We are intended to develop into some of His characteristics as well.

The meaning of these two words can further be understood by looking at Genesis 5:3.

> *When Adam had lived one hundred and thirty years, he became the father of a son in his own likeness, according to his image, and named him Seth* (Genesis 5:3).

Here Seth is said to be in the image and likeness of Adam, his father. These are the same two Hebrew words that are used in Genesis 1:26 when Scripture speaks of mankind being made in the image and likeness of God! Obviously Seth had many of Adam's characteristics but not all.

In the same way, mankind has many of God's qualities while no one possesses all of them. When we are compared to our heavenly Father, it's easy to see ourselves as flawed reflections and resemblances—as broken pots.

When we look at our families today, we can see many inherited traits, gifts, and inclinations. Children often resemble their parents physically, intellectually, spiritually, emotionally, and in their personalities.

I lived with my parents until I was in my twenties. We were a very close-knit family. For many years we traveled the country, going from one ministry to another, seeking a deeper understanding of the things of God. Our pursuit of God was a way of life. In this environment my love for God and His ways grew and increased. I learned to study the Scriptures for answers to my questions. My search for clarity continues today. Every time I read Scripture I ask, "Lord what have I not yet seen?"

Our journey through life is our opportunity to become more

and more like our heavenly Father. Just as we reflect and resemble our natural parents, so too are we intended to reflect and resemble God as His children.

Whose CAP Do We Wear?

God declared His intention for each of us in the first mention of man in Scripture as He announced that we are to be images and likenesses of Him. The Hebrew words translated "image" and "likeness" in the first chapter of Genesis can accurately be translated as "reflection" and "resemblance."

Reflection refers to the action of a mirror that reflects a source while appearing to have the source within. The appearance of God can be in us while the reflection that comes from us is only one dimensional. We are not intended to be or to act "as God."

Resemblance speaks of a similarity that usually entails character, attitude, and personality traits. No child of God can fully resemble our heavenly Father. No matter who we are, we all come up short of the reality that God is. Having some of the traits does not mean we are as the source. We are not and cannot be "as God."

God designed us to be and to function as apprentices who learn to reflect and resemble our heavenly Father as growing children. Our heavenly Father created mankind, you and me, to be children who would grow to reflect and resemble Him despite all our cracks and peculiarities.

The second chapter of Genesis tells us that when God brought the first man into existence, He formed a body out of natural realm material and infused it with an essence of spirit—of His life. The first man's soul consciousness emerged as he became a living being. It continued to grow and develop throughout his life.

Then the LORD God formed man of the dust of the ground, and breathed into his nostrils the breath of life; and man became a living being [soul] (Genesis 2:7).

Following the creation of the first person, God divided the one into two people, so they could participate in the birth and development of additional offspring.

And the LORD God fashioned into a woman the rib He had taken from the man, and brought her to the man (Genesis 2:22).

Now the man called his wife's name Eve, because she was the mother of all the living (Genesis 3:20-21).

We are all offspring of God and offspring of the first human parents. As such, we all have the same spirit, soul, and body make-up. This is why each of us is able to relate to and interact with both the natural and spiritual realities. The Apostle Paul verified our three-fold make-up when he prayed for us.

Now may the God of peace Himself sanctify you entirely; and may your spirit and soul and body be preserved complete, without blame at the coming of our Lord Jesus Christ (1 Thessalonians 5:23).

As offspring of God, we all have a deposit of His Spirit. We generally refer to this deposit as the spirit of life.

You hide Your face, they are dismayed; You take away their spirit, they expire and return to their dust (Psalm 104:29).

This spirit of life gives each of us the privilege of assisting God in the birth and development of His offspring. Each child born in this earth has natural parents *and* is an offspring of God. This also gives each of us the potential to become godly people. While we are all different, we have within us an inherent value that beckons us to be contributing members of the family of God.

Our heavenly Father views our differences as valuable variables.

> *Now there are varieties of gifts, but the same Spirit. And there are varieties of ministries, and the same Lord. There are varieties of effects, but the same God who works all things in all persons. But to each one is given the manifestation of the Spirit for the common good* (1 Corinthians 12:4-7).

God designed this earthly life to be a process for birthing and initially developing His offspring. Our earthly life is an on-going process that is designed to develop us as children into reflections and resemblances of our heavenly Father.

What is it in each of us that is able to reflect and resemble our heavenly Father? It's not our physical appearance. Nor is it because we can reason and feel, or because we can have understanding.

The greatest factor in us, which has the potential to reflect and resemble God, is found in the expression of our heart. Our heart expression is defined as the tri-fold capacities of character, attitude, and personality, or CAP. These qualities allow us to express a variety of perspectives, attitudes, and demeanors.

- **Character** is expressed in our moral fiber such as being pure, honest, kind, and loyal.

- **Attitude** is expressed in our temperament such as being humble or arrogant, flexible or stubborn.

- **Personality** is expressed in our social behavior such as in being creative, supportive, organized, and inspirational.

As beings, we are composed of a body, soul, and spirit. Our CAP expressions come from more than any one part of our being. They are a result of our composite being. In the book, *What Is Man?* we provide a detailed look at CAP and show that these attributes express our heart. Each of these expressions, in turn, helps define who we are as individuals.

Our heavenly Father desires that our character, attitude, and personality reflect and resemble His own heart expression. In Christ Jesus, God provided the most exact reflection and resemblance of His heart in a human life, so we could more clearly understand what He desires for our lives.

> *Do not lie to one another, since you laid aside the old self with its evil practices, and have put on the new self who is being renewed to a true knowledge according to the image of the One who created him* (Colossians 3:9-10).

> *For those whom He foreknew, He also predestined to become conformed to the image of His Son, so that He would be the firstborn among many brethren* (Romans 8:29).

Yes, we were all foreknown in the heart and mind of God. As such, we are intended to be conformed to the image God demonstrated two thousand years ago in a Son—Jesus Christ. His children are designed to resemble Him.

While people in the culture of Christ demonstrate many of the characteristics of children who are becoming Christ-like, even the most spiritual ones realize that in many ways, their CAP still falls short and is unlike Christ. There are areas in our heart that are still in transition and in some cases in need of radical change.

> *Since you...have put on the new self who is being renewed to a true knowledge according to the image of the One who created...put on a heart of compassion, kindness, humility, gentleness and patience; bearing with one another, and forgiving* (Colossians 3:12-13).

God changes not; but, as maturing children, our CAP is all about change. While there are areas in our CAP that are improving and becoming more Christ-like, there are also areas that are still shying away from God. Actually, we are both growing and dying simultaneously. We usually experience a little growing and a little dying in different areas of our life simultaneously as we put on the CAP of God.

Know His Ways

While our heavenly Father fully knows each of His offspring, He has always desired that we get to know Him so we can be blessed by the benefits of His ways among us.

When God gave the Ten Commandments to Israel He spoke to them face to face.

> *Then the LORD spoke to you* [Israel] *from the midst of the fire; you heard the sound of the words, but you saw no form—only a voice* (Deuteronomy 4:12).

The LORD spoke to you [Israel] *face to face at the mountain from the midst of the fire* (Deuteronomy 5:4).

The term "face to face" is taken from a Hebrew phrase that speaks of seeing a person from the front, the left, and the right, as though sight was three-dimensional. God saw Israel for who they were and really knew them inside and out. He knew about their shortcomings and thoroughly understood all their hang-ups.

As our heavenly Father fully knew Israel of old, He knows each of us, where we came from, and exactly where we are in our development. He knows about our cracks and cares for us anyway! Isn't He amazing?

Moses became as a savior to the people of Israel as God used him to facilitate all the miracles that delivered Israel from their Egyptian captivity. Following the miraculous deliverance and receiving the 10 Commandments, God said He knew and spoke to Moses face to face, as a friend.

Thus the LORD used to speak to Moses face to face, just as a man speaks to his friend (Exodus 33:11).

Scripture provides an interesting comparison between Moses and the people. Israel responded to God's efforts to share His guiding insight by asking Him to keep a distance and to communicate with them through a mediator—through Moses.

Then they said to Moses, "Speak to us yourself and we will listen; but let not God speak to us, or we will die" (Exodus 20:19).

When God said He spoke to Moses as a friend, we assume incorrectly that Moses also spoke to God as a friend. At this point in their relationship, Moses was a servant/minister in the hand of God. He did not know God very well. Moses responded to God's comment by asking Him to reveal His ways so he could get to know God personally.

> *Now therefore, I pray You, if I have found favor in Your sight, let me know Your ways that I may know You, so that I may find favor in Your sight* (Exodus 33:13).

Moses realized that if he knew God's thought patterns and was able to understand the reasons for His conduct, he would begin to really know Him as a friend. Moses wanted to know God beyond obedient service and miraculous activity. David tells us in the Psalms that God actually did make His ways known to Moses, but Israel was only able know the acts of God (see Psalms 103:7).

The acts of God refer to what He does while the ways of God speak of His reasoning thoughts and mannerisms. What a contrast! The people of Israel were satisfied with receiving God's blessings and miraculous interventions. Jesus spoke of this difference between servants and friends when He said:

> *You are My friends if you do what I command you. No longer do I call you slaves, for the slave does not know what his master is doing; but I have called you friends, for all things that I have heard from My Father I have made known to you* (John 15:14-15).

As a young man, travelling with my parents, I was exposed to many different Bible teachers. I remember getting irritated during one particular meeting. The minister kept saying, "You don't have to understand, just believe it." After several repetitions of this statement, a conviction gripped me. God gave us a mind so we could learn and begin to understand

Him and His ways. My desire to know and understand God was strengthened.

Scripture goes on to tell us the ways of God are right (Hosea 14:9), just (Daniel 4:37), blameless (Psalms 18:30), prosperous (Deuteronomy 28:9-14), holy (Psalms 77:13), and saving (Psalms 67:2).

These are the fruitful results and benefits of the ways of God. These outcomes are produced when the ways of God are functioning among us. The actual ways of God are the growth processes that God uses to help us change our ill perceptions and behaviors.

God's ways give us usable insight into why He deals with us as He does. They lend rhyme and reason to the processes that bring the results and benefits listed above. When we understand His ways, we are able to make more sense of His actions toward us. We want to understand that enjoying a few of these spill-over benefits of His ways is not the same as the life changing effects of knowing and walking in the ways of God.

Many of our harsh and insensitive attitudes and actions are a result of not understanding God's character and nature. God reveals much about Himself to people that participate in the culture of Christ. The chapters that follow will focus on different aspects of the revealed ways of God among us.

The ways of God provide the ways and means for us to develop, grow, and mature into better reflections and resemblances of His expressive heart. Our individual lives can be expressions of God, even in our cracked-pot imperfections.

Many ask if anyone can really know and understand the ways of God. Most of us have heard and can even quote one of the two Scriptures that tell us the thoughts and ways of God are beyond our comprehension. They are:

> *"For My thoughts are not your thoughts, nor are your ways My ways," declares the Lord. "For as the heavens are higher than the earth, so are My ways higher than your ways and My thoughts than your thoughts* (Isaiah 55:8-9).

> *Oh, the depth of the riches both of the wisdom and knowledge of God! How unsearchable are His judgments and unfathomable His ways* (Romans 11:33).

What are these verses saying? It helps to understand that in the Isaiah passage, God spoke to a rebellious Israel and in effect said they were so sadly lacking that they could not understand. God's thoughts and ways are beyond rebellious people. In the Romans verse Paul encouraged us to not settle for what we already know and understand. There is always more to understand for there is no end to our learning and our growing appreciation of God.

By the way, Scripture has much more to say about the ways of God. We are told 8 times that we can know the ways of God and 10 times that God wants to teach us His ways. Additionally, Scripture says we can keep the ways of God (5 times) and walk in the ways of God (20 times).

What a contrast to the idea that we cannot know! Why should we focus on the two passages that indicate God's ways are beyond us and ignore the other forty-three references? Each of the passages noted above are listed for your quick viewing in the Appendix.

See Appendix I: God Has Ways

Jesus gave us insightful clarity about this apparent scriptural contrast when He said:

> *Ask and it will be given to you; seek, and you will find; knock and it will be opened to you. For everyone who asks receives, and he who seeks finds, and to him who knocks it will be opened* (Matthew 7:7-8).

The ways of God are not beyond the understanding of those who seek. Everyone can seek to learn, know, understand, and even walk in the ways of God. Why settle for less?

Moses went from knowing God exists, to having encounters with Him, and then to being a faithful servant. Following Moses' request to know God's ways, God began to reveal His ways. As Moses began to understand and know God's ways, he became a great expression of the heart of his heavenly Father.

People in the culture of Christ are not satisfied with only knowing God as a help in our times of need. We want to know Him beyond miraculous interventions and beyond serving Him as Lord. Let's continue to ask, seek, and knock.

Life Develops

We are offspring of natural parents and a heavenly Parent. While God is our creative Father, our natural parents also play a major role in creating and raising us. God designed human life to work in such a way that natural and spiritual values are transmitted from one generation to the next.

We inherit our initial character traits, attitudes, and personalities from our natural parents. They introduce us to many basic qualities like cleanliness, neatness, sharing, and responsibility. We also receive our first clues about love and hate from them.

Our early experiences in life encourage us to embrace, struggle with, shy away from, or even reject our earthly parents' way of living. Because our natural parents are our first teachers, their good, bad, and indifferent parenting automatically taints our perceptions of our heavenly Father. Is God good, bad, or what? Can we count on Him to love and support us or is He like some of our earthly parents?

While our parents highly influence who we are and what we become, each of us choose how we respond to their examples. We decide what we accept and choose, what we will copy and duplicate. We then project what we have become onto our own children. Everyone around us is affected as well.

This life process is uniquely different for each of us. We all develop and mature into reflective resemblances of our earthly parents and of our heavenly Father in a variety of ways, at different rates, and into varying degrees of maturity. No one is an exact copy of either our earthly or our heavenly parent.

To the degree that we submit to God's love and partake of His fellowship in the culture of Christ, it is to that degree that we become shining expressions of His heart. Yes, we can actually become godly people during this life process. We really can know and walk in the ways of God. We can also teach them to our children so they can learn to reflect and resemble our heavenly Father, maybe even better than we have.

When we give ourselves to the ways of God that are experienced in the nutrient rich culture of Christ, we grow into better reflections and resemblances of His heart. God is faithful to lead and guide us into the abundance of life He designed us to live. He will do so to the degree that we give ourselves to seeking, knocking, and asking.

One day, a lawyer asked Jesus,

> *"Teacher, which is the great commandment in the Law?" And He said to him, 'You shall love the Lord your God with all your heart, and with all your soul, and with all your mind.' This is the great and foremost commandment. The second is like it, 'You shall love your neighbor as yourself.' On these two commandments depend the whole Law and the Prophets"* (Matthew 22:36-40).

In those days, the term "Law and the Prophets" meant all of written Scripture. Jesus was saying that all recorded Scripture is intended to help us develop into offspring that lovingly relate to both God and to one another. As we learn to fully love God and one another, we are learning to reflect and resemble our loving heavenly Father's heart.

It can be helpful to realize that every adjustment in our development usually comes one or two thoughts, feelings, or attitudes at a time. These changes progressively transform us into better cracked pots!

As we submit to God's loving care and partake of the fellowship of His presence, we learn to walk in His ways as His children. Even though each of us continues to appear as cracked pots, in the culture of Christ we are maturing into greater expressions of His heart, character, attitude, and personality (CAP).

As we give ourselves to the disciplines of the ways of God, we are empowered to partake of their benefits as the peaceable fruits of righteousness.

> *All discipline for the moment seems not to be joyful, but sorrowful; yet to those who have been trained by it, afterwards it yields the peaceful fruit of righteousness* (Hebrews 12:11).

In the meantime, we can all agree with the Apostle Paul who wrote a large portion of the New Testament. He admitted that each of us has room for improvement.

> *We all, with unveiled face, beholding as in a mirror the glory of the Lord, are being transformed* (2 Corinthians 3:16-18 and Romans 12:2).

> *Brethren, I do not regard myself as having laid hold of it yet; but one thing I do: forgetting what lies behind and reaching forward to what lies ahead, I press on toward the goal for the prize of the upward call of God in Christ Jesus* (Philippians 3:13-14).

God sent Moses to deliver Israel from slavery and lead them into a new way of life. (We will examine this in the next chapter.) That generation failed to go into the abundance that was promised, but the next generation after them accepted the challenge to follow God's lead and they became overcoming conquerors. Moses exhorted the willing:

> *So choose life in order that you may live, you and your descendants, by loving the LORD your God, by obeying His*

voice, and by holding fast to Him; for this is your life and the length of your days (Deuteronomy 30:19).

We want to remember that God has a purpose for each of our lives. He declared His purpose in the beginning. We are designed and intended to become godly people who reflect and resemble His heart in each of our situations and circumstances. However, we must choose this way of life. We choose to love, obey, and hold fast to Him.

In the culture of Christ, we're seeking, knocking, and asking about the ways of God among us. We're not satisfied with knowing Him as the Deity—as God. We want to know Him personally so we can become better reflections and resemblances of His heart.

Life is the journey God has designed for birthing and growing offspring into His image and likeness. In this inspirational culture of Christ, God among us teaches us His ways; and as children, we learn to reflect and resemble His heart. As we accept God's love and the fellowship of His presence, we grow into His heart's character, attitude, and personality.

Memorize Matthew 22:37-39:

> *And He said to him, "'You shall love the Lord your God with all your heart, and with all your soul, and with all your mind.' This is the great and foremost commandment. The second is like it, 'You shall love your neighbor as yourself.'"*

Questions to consider:

1. God declared His will for us in humanity's beginnings. What is it?

2. Who can know, understand, and walk in the ways of God?

3. Why is it important to view life as a developmental process?

Chapter 2

The Way of Salvation Transforms Us

There once was a farmer whose mule tripped and fell into a deep well. The farmer heard the mule braying but was unable to figure out how to get the animal out. It grieved him that he could not pull the animal out. The mule had been a good worker around the farm.

Although the farmer sympathized with the mule, he reluctantly called his neighbors together. He asked them to haul dirt to bury the old mule in the well and quietly put him out of his misery. At first, the mule was puzzled, but as the farmer and his neighbors continued shoveling dirt into the well, he had an idea: he ought to shake the dirt off his back and step on top of it. So he did just that.

"Shake it off and step up...shake it off and step up..." Despite the pain and the panic, the old mule just kept shaking off the dirt and stepping up! It wasn't long before the mule stepped over the lip of the well. What might have buried him became his means of escape, all because of the way he handled his adversity.

We understand that life is our personal growth journey. The life process initially births us into existence to experience growth cycles. While some cycles contain adversity and seem to be destructive, our heavenly Father uses them to mold us into reflections and resemblances of His heart of love.

Saved From Separation

At the beginning of human history, God made our first parents and placed them in the Garden of Eden. There He provided all they needed to grow and develop.

> *Out of the ground the LORD God caused to grow every tree that is pleasing to the sight and good for food; the tree of life also in the midst of the garden, and the tree of the knowledge of good and evil* (Genesis 2:9).

When God planted the tree of life and the tree of the knowledge of good and evil, He said both trees were pleasing to the sight and good for food. However, God gave Adam and Eve instructions that limited their choice.

> *The LORD God commanded the man, saying, "From any tree of the garden you may eat freely; but from the tree of the knowledge of good and evil you shall not eat, for in the day that you eat from it you will surely die"* (Genesis 2:16-17).

This Garden was filled with many good things to eat. When Adam and Eve chose to ignore our heavenly Father's instructions, they allowed another perception to become their guiding light.

When the woman saw that the tree was good for food, and that it was a delight to the eyes, and that the tree was desirable to make one wise, she took from its fruit and ate; and she gave also to her husband with her, and he ate. Then the eyes of both of them were opened (Genesis 3:6-7).

Their sin in the garden was not *what they did* as much as it was *what took place in their mind.* They accepted the deceptive temptation that they could ignore God, decide for themselves, and be "as God," which put them at odds with our heavenly Father and His purposes for their life.

Their decision to turn from God's instruction opened their eyes to see differently than He intended. They lost sight of God's love and intention. Instead of children, who were learning to reflect and resemble their heavenly Father, they began to think and act as though they were as God Himself.

The word translated "die" in 2:17 is a Hebrew indefinite (indicating "ing" belongs with the word). So this passage is saying, "For in the times you partake of the fruit of separation, you will be dying."

The decision produced in them, and consequently in humanity, a predominant separatist perception. When God came to communicate, they hid from His presence. Their newly adopted perception left them embarrassed and ashamed.

They heard the sound of the LORD God walking in the garden in the cool of the day, and the man and his wife hid themselves (Genesis 3:8).

Your iniquities have made a separation between you and your God, and your sins have hidden His face from you (Isaiah 59:2).

The deception "I am as God" separated them from God's insightful guidance. Ignoring God short-circuited their ability to see clearly and left them confused about His love. It also hindered their ability to live a godly life.

Their new "I am as God" perspective separated them from God's guiding fellowship. The sin nature we all inherit is really a result of our life apart from God's guidance. Our erroneous ways are the side effects of sin while our iniquities are multiplied side effects. It is a deadly way to live.

The story of the Prodigal Son graphically illustrates what separation from God's guidance is like.

And He said, "A man had two sons. The younger of them said to his father, 'Father, give me the share of the estate that falls to me.' So he divided his wealth between them. And not many days later, the younger son gathered everything together and went on a journey into a distant country, and there he squandered his estate with loose living" (Luke 15:11-13).

Without God in our lives, we tend to squander what He has given us. An example is found in the ideologies of communism and socialism. Their core idea of sharing is a biblical principle. However, when God is negated from the equation and the ideology is forced, it does not work.

The Prodigal story goes on to show the attitude of God's heart toward repentant children and to illustrate a from-death-back-to-life example of salvation.

And the son said to him, "Father, I have sinned against heaven and in your sight; I am no longer worthy to be called your son." But the father said to his slaves, "Quickly bring out the best robe and put it on him, and put a ring on his hand and sandals on his feet; and bring the fattened calf, kill it, and let us eat and celebrate; for this son of mine was dead and has come to life again; he was lost and has been found." And they began to celebrate (Luke 15:21-24).

When the older brother, who stayed at home, protested his father's gracious treatment of the Prodigal, the father explained the reason for his graciousness and rejoicing.

But we had to celebrate and rejoice, for this brother of yours was dead and has begun to live, and was lost and has been found (Luke 15:32).

The Apostle Paul mirrors this truth in a universal way.

And you were dead in your trespasses and sins, in which you formerly walked according to the course of this world, according to the prince of the power of the air, of the spirit that is now working in the sons of disobedience. Among them we too all formerly lived in the lusts of our flesh, indulging the desires of the flesh and of the mind, and were by nature children of wrath, even as the rest...

But God, being rich in mercy, because of His great love with which He loved us, even when we were dead in our transgressions, made us alive together with Christ (by grace you have been saved) (Ephesians 2:1-5).

The sin introduced in the Garden of Eden had little to do with what Adam and Eve did but more about the attitude change that came as they chose to separate from their Father's guidance. They chose to live as though they were God of their own life.

We inherit from our parents the seeds of separation, the same sinful tendency. Who has not dealt with the desire to do it my way? The question is: Do we water and nurture the erroneous seeds in us and give them any credibility?

Salvation is God's effort to restore us from sin's separation and reinstate us into His guiding fellowship. When we submit to His Lordship, we are saved from separation and we enter salvation's transforming way of life.

God Is Our Savior

Salvation is our heavenly Father's merciful initiative to restore us into His fellowship and save us from our wayward selves. God is the author of our salvation, the Savior who delivers from bondage to death's lifestyles.

> *Who has announced this from of old? Who has long since declared it? Is it not I, the Lord? And there is no other God besides Me, a righteous God and a Savior; there is none except Me. Turn to Me and be saved, all the ends of the earth; For I am God, and there is no other...*(Isaiah 45:21-22)

In the Old Testament, God sent Moses to Israel as His representative savior. He delivered them out of Egypt and led them into Canaan to be His disciplined children.

This Moses, whom they disowned, saying, "Who made you a ruler and a judge?" is the one whom God sent to be both a ruler and a deliverer with the help of the angel...This man led them out, performing wonders and signs in the land of Egypt and in the Red Sea and in the wilderness for forty years (Acts 7:35-36).

The salvation God provided for Israel involved more than deliverance from bondage. It released them from slavery to man's rule and gave them the freedom to follow His guiding presence into a new and better way of living. The story details how God's Way of Salvation is a process.

Then, in New Testament times, God sent His representative Savior for all mankind: Jesus Christ. This time God demonstrated more clearly that He is the One who saves.

We have seen and testify that the Father has sent the Son to be the savior of the world (1 John 4:14).

We have fixed our hope on the living God, who is the Savior of all men, especially of believers (1 Timothy 4:10).

Scripture says the blood shed on Calvary was really God's own life blood. God gave of Himself for us.

...whom God displayed publicly as a propitiation in His blood through faith. This was to demonstrate His righteousness, because in the forbearance of God He passed over the sins previously committed (Romans 3:25).

Blood represents the life of a person. When Christ shed His blood, it was as though God laid down His own life. Jesus did not save us from God's wrath as some tend to think. Jesus demonstrated God's love for us by showing that God does not condemn us but goes to great depths, lengths, and heights to restore us.

Our heavenly Father has openly demonstrated His love and care for us in the life of Christ. Now He beckons us to respond and come out of our deathly separation into the fellowship of His guiding presence in the culture of Christ. God invites all of us to be restored, taught, and disciplined into His way of living. Jesus said,

> *It is written in the prophets, "And they shall all be taught of God." Everyone who has heard and learned from the Father, comes to Me* (John 6:45).

> *Take My yoke upon you and learn from Me, for I am gentle and humble in heart, and you will find rest for your souls. For My yoke is easy and My burden is light* (Matthew 11:29-30).

When we partake of God's fellowship in the culture of Christ, we are more than inheritors of "someday." In God's fellowship, we can receive His eternal perspective and actually partake of an eternal quality of life.

> *Truly, truly, I say to you, he who believes has eternal life. I am the bread of life* (John 6:47-48).

> *Truly, truly, I say to you, he who hears My word, and believes Him who sent Me, has eternal life, and does not come into judgment, but has passed out of death into life* (John 5:24).

> *This is eternal life, that they may know You, the only true God, and Jesus Christ whom You have sent* (John 17:3).

Our heavenly Father so loves His offspring that He goes to all lengths to save us from our wayward selves. He wants us to know the same level of fellowship that Jesus demonstrated.

Saving Transitions

When God delivered Israel from their Egyptian bondage, they had lived as slaves for a few generations. While Israel wanted to be free, they didn't know how to govern themselves. Neither were they experienced at hearing God speak or following His guidance. They were conditioned to think as slaves. They had become dependent on their overlords to govern and provide for them.

God knew that deliverance, in itself, could not accomplish a lasting effect. They needed to learn how to think differently and how to function under His leadership.

> *Now it came about when Pharaoh had let the people go, that God did not lead them by way of the land of the Philistines, even though it was near; for God said, "Lest the people change their minds when they see war, and they return to Egypt"* (Exodus 13:17).

The wilderness journey was a necessary part of Israel's salvation. They needed time to transition from thinking and living as servants in order to become triumphant people. A time of transition would allow God to share His insight and teach them to live in the manner He designed developing children to live. A transition process would also help root out desires for the old life.

Yes, Israel's salvation involved more than deliverance. The Old Testament example of salvation reveals there are at least three major stages in the salvation process. First, we are initially delivered from what binds us to separation. Second, we go through transitions as we accept new ways of life under God's influence and put off old ways of thinking and living. Third, we begin to mature as children who freely live under God's guidance. The second and third stages are necessary in order to establish the first.

When we respond to the guiding light of God's love, we transform from being offspring, who do our own thing, into children who are being disciplined in the culture of Christ. We learn to reflect and resemble the character, attitude, and personality of God that was demonstrated in Jesus.

Israel's release from bondage began their time of transformation in the wilderness. This process would prepare them to live triumphantly in their new life. God intended their wilderness journey from Egypt to Canaan to be a two-year process. During this time, God proved they could count on Him. He provided life giving water out of a rock, food from the ground and sky (manna and quail), and even showed them victory in warfare.

Sadly, that generation failed to adjust what they felt and reasoned. Old attitudes limited their ability to really believe and enter into Canaan. They failed to receive all that God was providing to enter the fullness of their salvation. Nevertheless, God still loved and cared for them. He continued to provide miraculous food, water, and clothing for forty years. That generation fell short of God's intention and died in their transition.

As with Israel of old, we can be delivered and yet fail to enter into the fullness of life that God intends for us. We can decline transition and stall our transformation.

The culture of Christ helps us transition from our self-dependency into people who look to God for insightful guidance. As we put off the old ways and grasp a new life in Christ, we experience transition and begin to partake of eternal life.

Israel's wilderness transition was hindered by some of the same perceptions we entertain today.

1) Their faith was only in what their natural senses could see and hear.

> *Now when the people saw that Moses delayed to come down from the mountain, the people assembled about Aaron and said to him, "Come, make us a god who will go before us; as for this Moses, the man who brought us up from the land of Egypt, we do not know what has become of him"* (Exodus 32:1).

2) They believed they could not hear God speak.

> *Then they said to Moses, "Speak to us yourself and we will listen; but let not God speak to us, or we will die"* (Exodus 20:19). Also, see Deuteronomy 5:24-29.

3) They wanted God's help and miracles but would not accept the insights that would allow God to work through them.

> *The Lord said to Moses, "How long will this people spurn Me? And how long will they not believe in Me, despite all the signs which I have performed in their midst?"* (Numbers 14:11)

4) They also sought His miracles but rejected His presence.

> *They said to Moses, "Speak to us yourself and we will listen;*
> *but let not God speak to us, or we will die"* (Exodus 20:19).

How much are we remaining in our personal wilderness? Do we ignore the spiritual side of our senses that allow us to sense God speaking and leading? Do we treat His guiding presence as though it is for another dispensation or season? Do we refuse to die to our deathly habits and perceptions?

As developing offspring, we all choose to either receive or ignore God's guidance along life's pathway. The psalmist David spoke of this process when he wrote:

> *I will send an angel before you and I will drive out the*
> *Canaanite...for I will not go up in your midst, because you*
> *are an obstinate people, and I might destroy you on the*
> *way* (Exodus 33:2-3).

As with Israel of old, each of us needs to experience times of transition. These are seasons when we learn to live as God intends—when we shed deathly perceptions and accept God's perceptions, attitudes, and way of life.

Our personal salvation is never accomplished in one swooping action. Each of us transitions out of our old character, attitude, and personality (CAP) traits one thought, outlook, and expression at a time. Sometimes these changes are overlapping processes.

> *And do not be conformed to this world, but be transformed*
> *by the renewing of your mind, so that you may prove*
> *what the will of God is, that which is good and acceptable*
> *and perfect* (Romans 12:2).

In our heart and mind, transformation involves several transitions. It takes us time to allow what God has begun to become establish in us. We need to learn to think and feel differently so we can stop living as dead people separated from God.

Salvation Is a Process

Scripture teaches us that salvation is not a one-time event. Our restoration from sinful separation is an ongoing journey. The saving process helps us transition into relational intimacy with our heavenly Father.

But the path of the righteous is like the light of dawn, that shines brighter and brighter until the full day (Proverbs 4:18).

Make me know Your ways, O Lord; teach me Your paths. Lead me in Your truth and teach me, for You are the God of my salvation; for You I wait all the day (Psalm 25:4-5).

The Apostle Paul compares our saving growth process to that of an infant growing into maturity.

Therefore, putting aside all malice and all deceit and hypocrisy and envy and all slander, like newborn babies, long for the pure milk of the word, so that by it you may grow in respect to salvation (1 Peter 2:1-2).

As a result, we are no longer to be children, tossed here and there by waves and carried about by every wind of doctrine, by the trickery of men, by craftiness in deceitful scheming; but speaking the truth in love, we are to grow up in all aspects into Him who is the head, even Christ (Ephesians 4:14-15).

Paul also reminds us that it is our heavenly Father who is doing a lot of the work of bringing us into maturity.

For I am confident of this very thing, that He who began a good work in you will perfect it until the day of Christ Jesus (Philippians 1:6).

Work out your salvation with fear and trembling; for it is God who is at work in you, both to will and to work for His good pleasure (Philippians 2:12-13).

Sometimes what God is doing can seem like a judgment because it is hard on us. The ways of God are relatively easy on us when we cooperate with Him, but they become difficult when we do not.

As with Israel, God's mercy stays with us even if our transition is slow or we walk away for a time. The first trip to Canaan was a pleasure trip compared to the forty year burden when they refused to cooperate.

If you're hungry for more of God in your life, I have some good news: Salvation is more than one event, a past experience, a position we earn, or a stand we take. We take multiple steps, first in one area of life and then another. Our salvation comes in stages, through seasons, and by degrees. It reforms our thoughts, attitudes, and actions into more mature expressions of our heavenly Father's heart, day by day, season by season.

See Appendix II: Born Again

God provides many helps to assist our maturing growth. The following aids help keep us in salvation's pathway:

• Belief and confession (Romans 10:9-10)

• Baptism (1 Peter 3:21)

• The gift of faith (Luke 7:50; Ephesians 2:8)

• Washing of regeneration (Titus 3:5)

• Cleansing as by fire (1 Corinthians 3:15)

• The implanted Gospel (1 Corinthians 15:1-2; James 1:21)

• Jesus' life (John 3:17, 10:9; 1 Timothy 1:15; Romans 5:10)

• The name of the Lord (Acts 2:21; Romans 10:13)

• Our works (James 2:14-26)

• Our own sacrifice (Luke 9:23-24; John 15:8-13)

• One another's encouragement (Ephesians 4:15-16)

It is important to realize that each of these aids are helpful tools that God provides. Our salvation is not accomplished by the use of any one or two of these tools. Additionally, some tools may be more suitable for different people and in different situations.

We all tend to come up short of the character, attitude, and personality our heavenly Father revealed in Christ Jesus. Nevertheless, we get up each day and seek to be and to do better. We arise daily from death's slumbering ways, a little more than before. Then we go about the process of daily working out what God is working into us.

In reference to your former manner of life, you lay aside the old self, which is being corrupted in accordance with the lusts of deceit, and that you be renewed in the spirit of your mind, and put on the new self, which in the likeness of God has been created in righteousness and holiness of the truth (Ephesians 4:22-24).

Brethren, I do not regard myself as having laid hold of it yet; but one thing I do: forgetting what lies behind and reaching forward to what lies ahead, I press on toward the goal for the prize of the upward call of God in Christ Jesus (Philippians 3:13-14).

The choice our parents made in the Garden of Eden separated them from God's presence and produced deadly results. The ill effects of separation from God continually hinder our ability to grow into the people we are created to be.

Yes, we are in the world, but we do not have to be ruled by the world. Just as the old mule stuck in the well, let's shake off the deathly dust of the ways of separation and arise into the maturing lifestyle God desires for us.

It is in fellowship with our heavenly Father that our face becomes unveiled and we are able to see God's face more clearly. Our child-to-father fellowship allows Him to share with us His ways and teach us to live better lives.

Please remember, the original sin was ignoring God's guidance and His fellowship. This began the separation perspective that still complicates our lives today. We want to realize that everything is not "about me." (We will examine this in detail in the Way of Balance.)

As a great Father and loving Savior, God reaches out to deliver us from our bondage to deathly separation from His presence. The salvation God provides for our life involves many transitions. Each process we go through molds us so we can better reflect and resemble God's heart character, attitude, and personality. God provides salvation from our deathly lifestyle. His guiding presence in the culture of Christ assists our growth into His intention.

Memorize Philippians 3:13-14

Brethren, I do not regard myself as having laid hold of it yet; but one thing I do: forgetting what lies behind and reaching forward to what lies ahead, I press on toward the goal for the prize of the upward call of God in Christ Jesus.

Questions to Consider:

1. Which of the following ideas might hinder our spiritual journey? Why?

- I'm not worthy or good enough

- I said yes to God once

- I am saved just for heaven

- I don't need to change

- I can't hear God

2. Is salvation really an ongoing journey?

3. Are the following phrases appropriate or not? Why or why not?

- I'm saved.

- Are you saved?

- When were you saved?

Chapter 3

The Way of Forgiveness Restores Us

The Babemba tribe in southern Africa has learned something of the power of forgiveness to restore a tribal member from the error of his ways. When one of them violates the tribal code of conduct, they are placed unfettered in the center of the village. Life in the village comes to a halt as everyone— adults and children alike—gathers in a circle around the accused.

They do not pick up stones to cast at the offending tribal member. They do not speak a negative word against the guilty party; they do just the opposite! One by one, they take their turn sharing something good they can remember about the person. This is done loudly so everyone can hear. They recite the individual's good qualities, good deeds, strengths, and all the kindnesses the culprit has ever done in their lifetime.

This can go on for days, but no one is allowed to exaggerate, fabricate, or mock. At the end of the well-saying, the circle breaks up and everyone participates in a joyful celebration, welcoming the newly affirmed member back into the tribe! Anti-social, delinquent, and criminal behavior is rare among them. Why? They are masters at restoring the guilty one from the trespass that ensnared them.

We all experience the Way of Life because we are born into it. As we choose to respond to God and walk in the Way of Salvation, we experience the culture of Christ and begin to be transformed into God's intention. This saving process enables us to experience a more abundant life.

The Way of Forgiveness is an important foundational concept in the culture of Christ. Our proper function in this culture requires that we understand how God forgives so it becomes a primary basis for how we live.

In this chapter we focus on forgiveness from the standpoint of our heavenly Father, its originator. We will address such issues as: What motivates God to forgive? Who does God actually forgive? Are there limitations to His forgiveness? What is the real purpose of forgiveness?

As we examine scriptural examples of God's forgiveness, we will discover a lot about His heart and nature. We will begin to see more clearly our heavenly Father's character, attitude, and personality (CAP).

God Is Motivated

The words "forgive," "forgiven," and "forgiveness" appear in Scripture over one hundred times. The New Testament Greek word for "forgive," *aphiemi* (pronounced af-ee'-ay-mee), means to send away, dismiss, remove from another, liberate from the guilt and power of error.

The word "forgiveness," *aphesis,* means: remission, cause to stand away, release. This is an action that one exercises toward another, to accomplish a release in the recipient.

Forbearance says, "I'll give you one more chance." Forgiveness however says, "Let's forget it."

Scripture tells us that God *is* love! (See 1 John 4:8.) If God truly is love, then everything He does must be a result of His loving nature. We will begin to see this is really true.

When mankind was just a thought in God's heart and mind, before there was any need for forgiveness, the provision for our error was already in His loving essence.

> *...knowing that you were not redeemed with perishable things...but with precious blood, as of a lamb unblemished and spotless, the blood of Christ. For He was foreknown before the foundation of the world, but has appeared in these last times for the sake of you who through Him are believers in God* (1 Peter 1:18-20).

We can assume that God knew His offspring would err, for He knows all things. So if His intentions were to be realized, He had to have a remedy in mind. God was prepared! He has been a forgiver from the start. He is the greatest of all parents; His love overflows upon His offspring with an abundance of grace and mercy.

Adam and Eve did not repent of their sin, even when it was discovered. As an expression of His grace and mercy, God sent them out of the Garden, so they would not eat of the Tree of Life and remain unrepentant.

Too often we overlook the fact that He sent Jesus Christ into the world as a representation of His love. He did this to reveal His forgiveness and show us that His forgiving love is sufficient for each of us.

For God so loved the world, that He gave His only begotten Son, that whoever believes in Him shall not perish, but have eternal life (John 3:16).

God sent Jesus into the earth as His gift to proclaim, display, manifest, and demonstrate His forgiving heart. He revealed His deep love for us in a very personal way, in the life of Christ. No one can earn, win or purchase God's forgiveness; it is His loving gift to His offspring! His love for us is so great that He can't help Himself. What a Father!

His Love Is Full

The story is told of a minister who had sinned very badly and even though he had confessed his sin, he never felt forgiven.

A lady in his church was always saying, "The Lord said to me such and such." It wasn't that he didn't believe her, because she was usually right. It's just that she really irked him.

One day the minister said, "If God is speaking to you, ask Him to tell you what it was I did years ago."

A few days later, she came back to him. "Well?" he demanded. "Did you ask Him?"

"Yes," she replied.

"And what did He say?" asked the minister.

"He said He doesn't remember."

The minister's problem was a lack of understanding. If we do not really believe God's forgiveness is full and complete, we will not be able to feel its benefits.

You may wonder if it is really possible for God, who knows everything, to completely forgive and forget. This sounds like a real paradox. We can reasonably assume that God is able to do anything He wants because He is supreme. If God chooses not to keep an account of our errors, in essence what He has forgiven is no longer relevant—it is forgotten.

God provided a great view of His forgiving nature when He gave the Ten Commandments. After naming the first three (have no other gods, make no idol to represent, and do not profane His name), God paused to shed light on His heart of forgiveness.

> *For I, the LORD your God, am a jealous God, visiting the iniquity of the fathers on the children, on the third and the fourth generations of those who hate Me, but showing loving kindness to thousands, to those who love Me and keep My commandments* (Exodus 20:5-6).

When the Commandments are repeated in Deuteronomy, the same insight is shared after the second commandment.

> *For I, the LORD your God, am a jealous God, visiting the iniquity of the fathers on the children, and on the third and the fourth generations of those who hate Me, but showing loving kindness to thousands, to those who love Me and keep My commandments* (Deuteronomy 5:9-10).

In these verses, God compares His leaning toward forgiveness with His leaning toward justice. When the phrase "third and fourth generations" is compared with "thousands," Hebrew scholars say it demonstrates God's forgiveness is five hundred times greater than any leaning toward punishing justice. He really is a forgiver!

God said He prefers to restore through forgiveness than to rectify through punishment. God must have shared this insight with the Babemba tribe. The loving kindness that is resident in the gift of forgiveness is powerful.

For emphasis, the book of Exodus later expresses the insight again. This time the order is reversed and forgiveness is noted first.

> *Then the LORD passed by in front of him and proclaimed, "The LORD, the LORD God, compassionate and gracious, slow to anger, and abounding in loving kindness and truth; who keeps loving kindness for thousands, who forgives iniquity, transgression and sin; yet He will by no means leave the guilty unpunished, visiting the iniquity of fathers on the children and on the grandchildren to the third and fourth generations"* (Exodus 34:6-7).

The word "visiting" in this passage comes from the Hebrew *paqad*. This word has much to do with a higher power calling for a positive action. The word is used 285 times, first in Genesis 21:1 where the Lord intervened for Sara so she could bear Isaac. It is used 110 times in reference to a commander mustering troops. It is a constructive action, a call to adjust for a greater good. When God visits the iniquity of parents on children, it is His call to do better.

There is another insight hidden in these verses. The Hebrew

word *naqah* is translated "unpunished" and means "unclean." The scholar Zodhiates (in *The Hebrew-Greek Key Study Bible*) says this word means "to be clean, pure, and guiltless."

The concept of punishment in the Hebrew culture was different than what it means today. It was intended to correct the error with a remedy in order to clean up the mess. God actually said His remedy for our error was to clean us up. He said He would call us into right behavior even unto the third and fourth generation of error.

This is demonstrated in God's decree to Abram about the land of Canaan. God promised the land to Abraham's descendants because, as a people, the Canaanites still had opportunity to repent for their iniquity (commitment to sin) was not yet full (see Genesis 12:7; 15:16).

When the Israelites came from Egypt four generations later, God still had a witness in the land of Canaan, the Prophet Balaam (see Numbers 22:1-21).

Centuries later, God chides Israel for their lack of understanding of His corrective intent.

> *Yet you say, "Why should the son not bear the punishment for the father's iniquity?" When the son has practiced justice and righteousness and has observed all My statutes and done them, he shall surely live. The person who sins will die. The son will not bear the punishment for the father's iniquity, nor will the father bear the punishment for the son's iniquity; the righteousness of the righteous will be upon himself, and the wickedness of the wicked will be upon himself* (Ezekiel 18:19-20).

The only dark side of God is in our mistaken view of Him. Our misconception is even used as an excuse for our own bad behavior. After all, if God gets mad and bad things happen, why is it wrong for me to lose my temper?

See Appendix III: God's Judgments

Scripture is very clear concerning God's judgments. They are correcting disciplines that are always meant to help us:

> *You have forgotten the exhortation which is addressed to you as sons, "My son, do not regard lightly the discipline of the Lord, nor faint when you are reproved by Him; for those whom the Lord loves He disciplines, and He scourges every son whom He receives"* (Hebrews 12:5-6).

> *My son, do not reject the discipline of the LORD or loathe His reproof, for whom the LORD loves He reproves, even as a father corrects the son in whom he delights* (Proverbs 3:11-12).

God's forgiving nature is what motivates Him to forgive. His love for us is so full, He can't help Himself. He is always after what is best for us and for everyone else involved, even when we do not realize it. Too often the following verse is misunderstood:

> *In this is love, not that we loved God, but that He loved us and sent His Son to be the propitiation* [conciliatory allowance] *for our sins* (1 John 4:10).

God was not speaking of satisfying any problem He had with mankind. John was addressing man's misperception of how sin is really dealt with. They thought sacrifice was necessary to placate an angry God. He does not accept or respond to placating appeasement as though it might adjust what He thinks. He wants us to repent and change our mind regarding our ill activity.

No Reserve or Exceptions

In Spain, there was a father and a teenage son whose relationship had become so strained that the son ran away from home. His father, however, soon began to search for his rebellious, wayward son. Finally, after having exhausted all the possibilities, he made one last desperate effort to find his son. The father placed an ad in the Madrid newspaper. The ad read: "Dear Paco, meet me in front of the newspaper office at noon. All is forgiven. I love you. Please come home. Your father."

The next day, at noon, in front of the newspaper, 800 "Pacos" showed up—each one seeking forgiveness and love from his father.

—From *The Power of Forgiving* by Robert Strand

God's love for His offspring is stronger and purer than any parent's love. His love looks beyond the error of His offspring and continually calls each of us into the loving care and support of His fellowship.

Our heavenly Father is a forgiver, first and foremost.

> *Who is a God like You, who pardons iniquity and passes over the rebellious act of the remnant of His possession? He does not retain His anger forever, because He delights in unchanging love. He will again have compassion on us; He will tread our iniquities under foot. Yes, You will cast all their sins into the depths of the sea* (Micah 7:18-19).

He is faithful and righteous to forgive us our sins and to cleanse us from all unrighteousness (1 John 1:9).

I, even I, am the one who wipes out your transgressions for my own sake; and I will not remember your sins (Isaiah 43:25).

How could God possibly forgive for His own sake? Consider for a moment: God loves every one of His offspring, yet the vast majority go astray. If God did not forgive, He could feel some of the heartbreak that usually accompanies not forgiving: guilt, shame, anger, and bitterness. Instead, God's forgiving nature keeps Him free of such haunting and degrading side effects.

God even admonishes us to not lose heart when things continue to be difficult.

For consider Him who has endured such hostility by sinners against Himself, so that you will not grow weary and lose heart (Hebrews 12:3).

Jesus demonstrated God's forgiving love during His crucifixion when He prayed with the heart of His Father.

Father, forgive them; for they do not know what they are doing (Luke 23:34).

God's love for us is so full that it spills over into our lives. His heart of love directs His actions toward His offspring and His disciplined children. He does not want to leave any of us separated from His loving care.

To illustrate the forgiving character of our heavenly Father, Jesus told the story of the Prodigal Son.

And He said, "A man had two sons. The younger of them said to his father, 'Father, give me the share of the estate that falls to me…' And not many days later, the younger son gathered everything together and went on a journey into a distant country, and there he squandered his estate with loose living…" (Luke 15:11-13).

But when he came to his senses, he said, "How many of my father's hired men have more than enough bread, but I am dying here with hunger!"…So he got up and came to his father. But while he was still a long way off, his father saw him and felt compassion for him, and ran and embraced him and kissed him (Luke 15:17, 20).

And the son said to him, "Father, I have sinned against heaven and in your sight; I am no longer worthy to be called your son." But the father said to his slaves, "Quickly bring out the best robe and put it on him, and put a ring on his hand and sandals on his feet; …for this son of mine was dead and has come to life again; he was lost and has been found" (Luke 15:21-22, 24).

The son took the livelihood his father provided and squandered it. The father, however, continued to love his wayward offspring. This becomes obvious when we see the father accepted the son even before he heard the son repent. So it is with God—He readily welcomes us into His loving care.

It is important for us to understand God's forgiveness is not passive. Jesus said this father ran to embrace his son before he repented. *The Message Bible* records God's grace in Romans 5:20 as "aggressive forgiveness." God's forgiveness is not dependent on us. He gives it willingly and without reserve. Our problem lays in our lack of sincere repentance. We receive the full benefits of God's forgiveness by repenting and turning toward changing our ways.

We also want to realize there is nothing God does not forgive. The only hint in Scripture of a limitation to God's forgiveness is found in only one passage.

> *Truly I say to you, all sins shall be forgiven the sons of men, and whatever blasphemies they utter; but whoever blasphemes against the Holy Spirit never has forgiveness, but is guilty of an eternal sin* (Mark 3:28-29).

What is this verse actually saying? Many times we have to look beyond the obvious to see the truth in a matter. One of the reasons the Holy Spirit comes is to convict of sin (see John 16:8). When we refuse to be convicted and repent of error, we act as though the Holy Spirit is not worth heeding and God is ignored. Such action, in essence, slanders and blasphemes the Holy Spirit.

The word "eternal" in the above verse does not mean without beginning or end, it means "ongoing." There are no restrictions or limitations to God's forgiveness. But as long as we refuse to repent and receive His forgiveness, we choose to remain unforgiven. Thus we remain in our sin. We can, as illustrated by the minister we noted, not understand how fully God forgives and continue to live with guilt as unforgiven.

Restored To Become

Forgiveness is God's open invitation for us to repent and return to His guiding presence. His love dominates His nature so much that He does not dwell on our error.

But God, being rich in mercy, because of His great love with which He loved us, even when we were dead in our transgressions, made us alive together with Christ (by grace you have been saved) (Ephesians 2:4-5).

Straightening up, Jesus said to her, "Woman, where are they? Did no one condemn you?" She said, "No one, Lord." And Jesus said, "I do not condemn you, either. Go. From now on sin no more" (John 8:10-11).

God harbors no desire to condemn anyone. His forgiving nature is what causes His compassion, grace, mercy, and loving kindness to flow toward us, without exception. God continually seeks our restoration. He has no desire to leave any of us in our mess.

We can now understand how God's grace, compassion, and overwhelming desire to be merciful come from His forgiving heart. Jesus Christ revealed, proclaimed, displayed, demonstrated, and manifested God's gift of forgiveness so we could better understand His love for us and be drawn to Him.

Our heavenly Father is the embodiment of love. It defines who He is and guides His actions. God's undying love and eternal view of His intention for us, allows Him to see beyond our separating activity. This is not to indicate that God does not see our imperfections and shortcomings. As a great Father, He is just patiently diligent. He continually calls us to enter His fellowship and receive the benefits of His forgiving love. He wants us to grow up and become better children.

God wants us to get to know Him intimately as our heavenly Father. He doesn't want anyone's growth to be stunted, nor for any us to remain immature. Forgiveness is an extension of

His heart of love, His invitation for us to repent and enter His fellowship.

> *Or do you think lightly of the riches of His kindness and tolerance and patience, not knowing that the kindness of God leads you to repentance?* (Romans 2:4)

Jesus came to make the culture of Christ more visible in the earth. The coming of Christ 2,000 years ago brought such clarity that multitudes began to partake. It was reported that partakers of this Culture "upset the known world" (see Acts 17:6). They were generally referred to as people of faith. Their gathering as people became known as the kingdom of God "among us."

> *For the kingdom of God is not eating and drinking, but righteousness and peace and joy in the Holy Spirit* (Romans 14:17).

Forgiveness is God's non-condemning invitation for us to enter His insightful fellowship. Each of us can partake of His guidance and be restored from our wayward separation. God's forgiveness is absolute, but to receive it and partake of its benefits, we must become repentant people. We will address repentance in the next chapter.

God's way of forgiving is foundational to the culture of Christ. Yes, we can learn to reflect and resemble His heart's character, attitude, and personality (CAP).

God is the embodiment of love. Love defines who He is and guides His actions. His love for us is so full that He forgives us without reserve. God's merciful forgiveness is our invitation to repent and enter the culture of Christ, to experience

God among us. We can find release from our bondage and learn to respond to His guiding presence.

Memorize Exodus 34:6

> *Then the Lord passed by in front of him and proclaimed, "The Lord, the Lord God, compassionate and gracious, slow to anger, and abounding in lovingkindness and truth."*

Questions to Consider:

1. How does God's forgiveness compare to His leaning toward justice?

2. How can God, who knows everything, forget our sin?

3. What expressions of God's love add depth to His forgiving nature?

Chapter 4

The Way of Repentance Releases Us

If you put a buzzard in a pen that is 6 feet by 8 feet and entirely open at the top, in spite of its ability to fly, the bird will be an absolute prisoner. The reason is that a buzzard always begins a flight from the ground with a run of 10 to 12 feet. Without space to run, as is its habit, it will not even attempt to fly. He will remain a prisoner in a small jail with no top.

The ordinary bat that flies around at night, a remarkable nimble creature in the air, cannot take off from a level place. If it is placed on the floor or flat ground, all it can do is shuffle about helplessly until it reaches some slight elevation from which it can throw itself into the air. Then, at once, it takes off like a flash.

A bumblebee, if dropped into an open tumbler, will be there until it dies unless it is taken out. It never sees the means of escape at the top. It will persist in trying to find a way out through the sides. It will seek a way where none exists until it destroys itself.

In many ways, people are like the buzzard, the bat, and the bumblebee. We struggle with our problems and frustrations, continuing to act and do as we have always done. We fail to realize that all we have to do is look up and make an adjustment each time we find ourselves caught in a mess!

Repentance is the activity of admitting our need to adjust our attitude and actions. Our heart-felt repentance prepares us to adapt and learn to approach situations differently.

The eight ways of God we experience in the culture of Christ are the systematic processes that bring us into God's intention for our life. These processes help us grow and transform so we can better reflect and resemble our heavenly Father's heart.

In the last chapter we learned that God's way of forgiving can restore us from our captivity to sin's separation. We now understand that forgiveness is God's open invitation for us to escape into the freedom of salvation's transforming way.

An invitation, however, does not mean we automatically receive what God gives or that offspring routinely become children who are disciplined by Father. We must choose to partake of salvation's transformations. We do so by repenting.

We Maintain Separation

A good friend of mine has a relative who rebelled against his parents in his early teens. This caused a breach in their relationship. His rebellious self-will eventually led him into the illegal drug culture. As he grew further and further away from his parents, his life began to spin out of control. He went from being a user to a dealer. The law finally caught up with him and he spent the next twelve years in prison.

A broken and dysfunctional family resulted from this person's misguided desire to be the "king" of his life.

A different king, David, observed this same attitude.

> *If a man does not repent...Behold, he travails with wickedness, and he conceives mischief and brings forth falsehood. He has dug a pit and hollowed it out, and has fallen into the hole which he made. His mischief will return upon his own head, and his violence will descend upon his own pate* (Psalm 7:12, 14-16).

When our first parents chose to ignore the instructions of God, as promised, deathly perspectives took hold.

> *The LORD God commanded the man, saying, "From any tree of the garden you may eat freely; but from the tree of the knowledge of good and evil you shall not eat, for in the day that you eat from it you will surely die"* (Genesis 2:16-17).

> *Therefore, just as through one man sin entered into the world, and death through sin, and so death spread to all men* (Romans 5:12).

As Adam and Eve ignored God's guidance and chose self-rule, their perceptions of life distorted. Their newly acquired "I am as God" attitude clouded their ability to relate to God as their loving heavenly Father. It also complicated their relationship with each other.

This distorted attitude toward life caused them to begin to live separated from God, as spiritually dead people. A dreadful fear overcame what had once been a reverent awe of God.

And they heard the sound of the LORD God walking in the garden in the cool of the day, and the man and his wife hid themselves from the presence of the LORD God among the trees of the garden (Genesis 3:7-8).

As they crowned themselves god, a self-centered attitude began to rule their thoughts. They began to cover-up in each other's presence and hide from God. Our forgiving God came to fellowship with them, even in their rebellion. Instead of repenting, they hid from His revealing presence.

Then the LORD God called to the man, and said to him, "Where are you?" He said, "I heard the sound of You in the garden, and I was afraid because I was naked; so I hid myself" (Genesis 3:9-10).

Adam's further effort to deal with the guilt of his error was to blame God for giving him Eve.

The man said, "The woman whom You gave to be with me, she gave me from the tree, and I ate" (Genesis 3:10).

And the blame game begins! Everyone else is at fault here. We make excuses rather than repent. In God's presence, the "God complex" does not seem to work very well as an excuse for our own ill behavior.

Since they were unrepentant, God removed them from the Garden. He did not want them to eat of the Tree of Life and continue to live with the separating attitude.

Then the LORD God said, "Behold, the man has become like one of Us, knowing good and evil; and now, he might stretch out his hand, and take also from the tree of life, and eat, and live forever"—therefore the Lord God sent him out from the garden of Eden, to cultivate the ground from which he was taken. So He drove the man out; and at the east of the garden of Eden He stationed the cherubim and the flaming sword which turned every direction to guard the way to the tree of life (Genesis 3:22-24).

Removal from the Garden's Tree of Life was really an extension of His grace and mercy. God gave them time and space to begin to desire His guidance and become repentant. Their so-called punishment was to live in the separating death they chose.

In death's separation, we also hide and cover-up. We follow Adam's lead and make excuses: "It's not my fault; the devil made me do it." Anyone else or anything else is to blame—I'm not really at fault. I'm the victim here. The victim mentality shifts blame to excuse our dysfunction. As we maintain our separatist position and refuse to repent, we continue to obscure God's face from our view.

Your iniquities have made a separation between you and your God, and your sins have hidden His face from you (Isaiah 59:2).

Our lack of repentance keeps us captive to destructive thoughts, attitudes, and actions. Our unrepentant separation is the real problem. It even keeps us fearing that God will punish us because we are bad. We bring many ills upon ourselves by continuing to dig afresh our pits of destruction.

Scripture clearly tells us the judgments of God are corrective, not punitive. God is looking for good results.

It is for discipline that you endure; God deals with you as with sons; for what son is there whom his father does not discipline? (Hebrews 12:7)

I will be a father to him and he will be a son to Me; when he commits iniquity, I will correct him with the rod of men and the strokes of the sons of men (2 Samuel 7:14).

God's heart is so full of forgiving mercy that He constantly pursues us to repent and receive His guidance. God has no desire to leave us in our error. When we refuse to repent, God's continual pursuit of us may even begin to appear as harsh judgments.

Separation from God is what produces the deathly lives we live. When we repent and turn from our deadly lifestyles, we reverse our efforts to die in our mess. We need to remember that God is our loving heavenly Father. He wants us to grow and learn to reflect and resemble His heart character, attitude, and personality (CAP).

Death Cycle Altered

Jack (not his real name) grew up in a Christian home. He lost his faith as a lad and turned to atheism and the occult. He was well read, creative, intellectually brilliant, and was even awarded a scholarship to Oxford. Jack was called to serve in the First World War and seeing the horrors of war confirmed his atheism. Eventually he became a published author.

When he was 32 years old, he repented and returned to faith in God due to the influence of a close friend who was also a writer. Jack's renewed faith had a profound affect on his writing, so much so that he was to become known as one of the most famous defenders of the Christian faith. His real name is Clive Staples Lewis or as he is commonly known, C.S. Lewis. His close friend was J.R.R. Tolkien.

Repentance comes from the Greek, *metanoia*, and means to have another mind, think differently, turn around; a complete turning from a former understanding, attitude, state of being and action; to think and do differently. This is exactly what C.S. Lewis experienced.

The act of repentance, as the Greek defines it, is much more than an acknowledgment of error; it includes a turning from error with a complete change of perspective, attitude, and actions. You might call repentance the ultimate paradigm shift. Feeling remorse, being sorry, or fearing punishment are only preparations for real repentance.

Our word "metamorphosis," comes from the same Greek root as repentance. Metamorphosis describes the experience of a lowly caterpillar changing into a beautiful butterfly. When a caterpillar's state of being is no longer appropriate, it stops the former activity and wraps itself in a cocoon (a change process). Transformation comes as it goes through internal and external changes.

As the transformed creature emerges, its ground-level quality of life is left behind. It experiences life from a higher elevated perspective as a butterfly.

Again, when a wicked man turns away from his wickedness which he has committed and practices justice and righteousness, he will save his life (Ezekiel 18:27).

"Cast away from you all your transgressions which you have committed and make yourselves a new heart and a new spirit! For why will you die, O house of Israel? For I have no pleasure in the death of anyone who dies," declares the LORD God. Therefore, repent and live" (Ezekiel 18:29-32).

When we repent, we begin to reject our erroneous ways and turn from them. We seek to be different and learn to be a new person. This is how we, with God's help, change ourselves and make our heart and spirit new.

Sincere repentance brings an internal and external metamorphosis. We change what we think, believe, desire, and do. Our repentance releases us from our debilitating separation. It allows God's forgiving mercy and enabling grace to help us "go and sin no more." Yes, His grace does great things!

Repentance is the pivotal action that turns us toward our heavenly Father and the eternal perspective He provides. When we repent, we begin to see God more clearly and are able to partake of the culture of Christ. Our repentance is what allows us access to the Tree of Life.

Our refusal to become repentant people who seek to change our way of living is the one thing that keeps us from receiving the full benefits of God's forgiveness. When we repent, we are released from death's hold on our attitude and are able to learn to live life anew. We position ourselves to receive the forgiveness God has given. Our repentant heart equips us to partake of the fuller benefits of salvation's restoring mercy, enabling grace, and guiding insight.

Humble Action

A man named Bruce adapted a few perceptions early in life that made marriage and family life very difficult. Eventually divorce resulted. Bruce then left the area and had no contact with his family for a few years. When Bruce returned to the area, he attended church services where his former wife, Diana, attended. Neither made any effort to talk. Before long, his presence in the meetings began to seriously irritate Diana.

When she asked for help, the pastor suggested a remedy. The next time Bruce came to a meeting, she was to take him aside and sincerely ask him to forgive her for the divorce. The minister said his reaction would be a pleasant surprise.

Diana argued that she was not the problem; he was the one that made everything unbearable. But since Diana was a rather humble person, she decided to do it. At the next opportunity, Diana approached Bruce and asked him for forgiveness.

Bruce immediately said, "No, no, it was entirely my fault. You did nothing wrong. Will you forgive me?"

She was flabbergasted. Never before had Bruce admitted anything was his fault; it was always someone or something else—a bad spirit, the devil, the kids, or Diana herself.

Diana said it felt like a heavy weight dropped from her shoulders. She was released from the guilt she carried over the divorce. Her irritations about Bruce and his presence in the meetings also ceased.

When we humbly repent and set our hearts right before God and one another, we allow God to remove any guilt, anger, or bitterness we have been carrying. A repentant person can even apologize for being at odds with someone. We will seek restoration, no matter who was right or wrong.

> *Therefore if you are presenting your offering at the altar, and there remember that your brother has something against you, leave your offering there before the altar and go; first be reconciled to your brother, and then come and present your offering* (Matthew 5:23-24).

Our repentant acceptance of responsibility for being at odds invites others to be restored. We want to be contrite people who are quick to humbly repent. When we accept responsibility, admit error, and repent, it cuts through any pride in us.

Pride wants to protect who we are at all costs and will argue a point to prove superiority. Our god-complex uses pride to withstand most any probing question that might generate conviction. Pride openly despises anything that might encourage us to repentance. The contrast between pride and humility is very great.

The most powerful counter to our pride is to acknowledge error and humbly repent. A humble person tends to be quick to repent and accept responsibility. Both the Old and New Testaments speak of humility and repentance as though they are closely connected.

See Appendix IV: The Power of Humility

Humility speaks of our state of being, while repentance is an activity of the humble. This is why the humble person is quick to repent even if not fully at fault. To admit and repent of personal error is a very humbling activity. When we humbly repent, God's favor assists our efforts to change.

But He gives a greater grace. Therefore it says, "God is opposed to the proud, but gives grace to the humble." ...humble yourselves in the presence of the Lord, and He will exalt you (James 4:6, 10).

Repent therefore and return, that your sins may be wiped away, in order that times of refreshing may come from the presence of the Lord; and that He may send Jesus, the Christ appointed for you (Acts 3:19-20).

God not only gives greater grace to the humbly repentant person, He also blesses them with times of refreshing in His presence. He even exalts them in appropriate ways.

In our ignorance, we believe that if we make sacrifices and give gifts (as under the Law), everything will be fine. When we continue down our prideful, self-destructive paths, God is clear—He dislikes our sacrifice and offering.

Bring your worthless offerings no longer, incense is an abomination to Me...I hate your new moon festivals and your appointed feasts, they have become a burden to Me; I am weary of bearing them. So when you spread out your hands in prayer, I will hide My eyes from you; Yes, even though you multiply prayers, I will not listen. Your hands are covered with blood. Wash yourselves, make yourselves clean; Remove the evil of your deeds from My sight. Cease to do evil, learn to do good (Isaiah 1:13-17).

While bringing restitution is a good thing, God wants us to turn from our error and embrace His thoughts and attitudes. A repentant person is humble. Humble repentance powerfully releases us into our heavenly Father's fellowship and a better life, reversing our deathly separation. Our humble repentance invites God's compassionate mercy and enabling grace, and gives us a peaceful rest from the strife and anxieties of discord.

Repentance and Health

God's forgiveness extends His grace and mercy even while we are in error. Grace is getting what we don't deserve while mercy is not getting what we do deserve.

As a wonderful Father, God delights in cleaning us up if we are willing to cooperate. Forgiveness does not excuse error but is God's invitation for us to repent and partake of His fellowship in the culture of Christ.

When Jesus responded to the faith that people exercised, He made a connection between forgiveness and healing.

> *Which is easier, to say to the paralytic, "Your sins are forgiven"; or to say, "Get up, and pick up your pallet and walk"? But so that you may know that the Son of Man has authority on earth to forgive sins, He said to the paralytic, "I say to you, get up, pick up your pallet and go home"* (Mark 2:9-11).

Several years ago a minister went to Ireland for a crusade. His preaching and healing miracles brought many commitments to Christ. The next year he returned, experienced great success, and rescheduled again. As he ministered the third year, he recognized many of the people coming for prayer were those who previously received healing. He asked God why they were losing what He had given.

God revealed that they continued to think and do what originally made them sick. A few years later this minister returned to reside and teach them about healthy eating and exercise.

God loves to intervene and forgivingly heal our physical diseases and emotional hurts. However, if He heals us and we fail to change our ways, it could be assumed that God is supporting our error.

Many times we ask God to heal and deliver and then wonder why He doesn't. Why should He heal if we persistently think and do what originally caused the problem? If He heals and we continue in our physical, mental, or emotional error, we dig afresh our pits of destruction. This insight into God's heart of forgiveness does not insinuate that all sickness or defects are a result of sinful error. We are just pointing out that much of our sickness is a result of a lack of repentant change.

There are many reasons we get sick. Some illnesses are known to strengthen our physical immune system. These occasions actually support long-term health. Other times sickness is a result of accidents and unfortunate circumstances.

Jesus gave us an example to clarify the issue:

> *His disciples asked Him, "Rabbi, who sinned, this man or his parents, that he would be born blind?" Jesus answered, "It was neither that this man sinned, nor his parents; but it was so that the works of God might be displayed in him"* (John 9:2-3).

God's forgiving grace and mercy are readily available. Our enjoyment of them, however, can depend on our willingness to repent and change our perceptions and actions. Our lack of such willingness is generally what keeps us from receiving the full benefits of God's salvation. We need to look up, just like the buzzard, bat, and bumblebee.

The only right way to approach our heavenly Father is as a humble, repentant child. Humble children are able to partake of His life-giving fellowship and enjoy times of refreshing in His presence where His forgiving mercy and enabling grace assist our efforts to change.

In the culture of Christ, we learn to humbly repent and become repentant people. Repentant people do more than repent, they are humble enough to quickly admit error and are open to improving change.

The Way of Repentance helps us learn how to better reflect and resemble our heavenly Father's heart character, attitude and personality (CAP) as it is revealed in Christ.

Memorize Acts 3:19-20:

> *Therefore repent and return, so that your sins may be wiped away, in order that times of refreshing may come from the presence of the Lord; and that He may send Jesus, the Christ appointed for you,*

Questions to Consider:
1. What is the difference between asking for forgiveness and repenting?

2. If God has already forgiven, why do we need to repent?

3. What does God really want from us when we err?

Chapter 5

The Way of Change Adjusts Us

There was once a man who had four sons. He wanted his sons to learn not to judge things too quickly. So he sent them each on a quest, in turn, to go and look at a pear tree that was a great distance away.

The first son went in the winter, the second in the spring, the third in summer, and the youngest son in the fall. When they had all returned, he called them together to describe what they had seen.

The first son said, "The tree was ugly, bent, and twisted."

The second son said, "No, it was covered with green buds and full of promise."

The third son disagreed; he said, "It was laden with blossoms that smelled so sweet and looked so beautiful, it was the most graceful thing I have ever seen."

The last son disagreed with all of them; he said, "It was ripe and drooping with fruit, full of life and fulfillment."

The man then explained to his sons that they were all right because they had each seen only one season in the tree's life. He told them that you cannot judge a tree or a person, by only one season. He said the essence of who we are and the pleasure, joy, and love of life can only be measured by looking at all the seasons.

If we give up when it's winter, we will miss the promise of our spring, the beauty of our summer, and the fulfillment of our fall. We don't want to settle for the season we are in because each change of season helps us to grow.

The Ways of God experienced in the culture of Christ are more than good ideas or values. They are processes that help us grow and mature as children of God. The ways of God are processes that mold and shape us into people who reflect and resemble the character, attitude, and personality of God's heart.

Let's take a moment to recap what we have observed in the first four chapters.

In chapter 1, we observed how the Way of Life is a life-long process that God uses to initially birth His offspring into existence, and then to grow and develop us.

In chapter 2, we found the Way of Salvation is the transformational process that God uses to change offspring into children who pursue His guiding presence.

In chapter 3, we saw the Way of Forgiveness is God's invitational effort to restore us into His fellowship and release us from the attitudes that maintain our separation.

The first three chapters speak of God's fatherly heart. We get a good look at His love for His offspring and begin understanding His desire to assist our growing development. He constantly invites us to receive His guiding insight so we can reflect and resemble His heart more appropriately.

In chapter 4, the Way of Repentance reveals how we receive the full benefits of His forgiveness. A lot of our freedom to grow is dependent on our willingness to repent and change.

The next four chapters (5-8) will continue to focus on our response to the guidance God provides for His children in the culture of Christ. Each of the Ways of God progressively leads us into greater levels of maturity as children of God.

Create and Make

God is the Eternal One who existed before the created natural universe of time and space. Since He created the natural progressions, He is not limited or contained by them. He does not grow or adjust by any progression.

Because I have spoken, I have purposed, and I will not change My mind, nor will I turn from it (Jeremiah 4:24).

For I, the Lord, do not change; therefore you, O sons of Jacob, are not consumed (Malachi 3:6).

While God does not change, His spoken expression enters into time and space to bring about change.

So will My word be which goes forth from My mouth; it will not return to Me empty, without accomplishing what I desire, and without succeeding in the matter for which I sent it (Isaiah 55:11).

God's spoken word goes forth with three distinctive creative features: a designed intention, an action plan to implement it, and the ability to make it so.

See Appendix V: Agent of Change

When the changeless One designed and created the natural universe, He implemented an entire realm of change.

> *Of old You founded the earth, and the heavens are the work of Your hands. Even they will perish, but You endure; and all of them will wear out like a garment; like clothing You will change them and they will be changed. But You are the same, and Your years will not come to an end* (Psalm 102:25-27).

From God's eternal perspective, what He says is as good as done. He said it; so it will be. In the earth, however, there is a beginning and then a forming process to make and establish what He creates into a full reality.

In the natural realm, fulfillment of God's desire usually involves a progression of time, with beginnings that are followed by "making and forming" processes. Many things may need to change before His spoken will is established. The ever moving natural universe is designed and ordered in such a way that it will continue to experience change through all the progression of time.

The first chapter of Genesis gives us a limited look at what is known as the creation week. With very little detail, it tells of six creative days. The first three verses of chapter two finishes the account of the creation week with a seventh day of rest.

This creation account tells of God forming the earth, composing its atmosphere, and creating natural life forms. On the sixth day, God brings into existence His offspring—mankind.

Then God said, "Let Us make man in Our image, according to Our likeness..." God created man in His own image, in the image of God He created him; male and female He created them (Genesis 1:26-27).

This chapter is only a glimpse into how the natural creation came into existence. In these two verses about man, God creates "one man" and then He identifies a "them," without giving any detail as to how this was accomplished. More details come in the next chapter when God shares how He made the man and them.

The six days of creation are wrapped up in this verse:

Thus the heavens and the earth were completed, and all their hosts (Genesis 2:1).

The word "hosts" in this verse comes from the Hebrew *tasba*. This word is used often to speak of a mass of people but never of animals. So this first account of the creation week includes the hosts of God's offspring that are noted in Genesis 1:26-27.

It is common in Hebrew writing to give an overview and then retell a section of it with more detail while focusing on certain aspects. We do this today when we announce a subject and then elaborate with much detail.

It can be helpful to notice a few translation irregularities:

The Hebrew word *yowm* is translated "day" in the first and second chapters of Genesis. Yowm actually means "cycle." It can speak of a 24 hour day, and it is also used to speak of an unspecified time frame.

An example is found in the comment that previews the second account. This verse speaks of the seven cycles (days) of creation as though they were one creative cycle (day).

> *This is the account of the heavens and the earth when they were created, in the day* [yowm-cycle] *that the LORD God made earth and heaven* (Genesis 2:4).

The use of yown in this verse actually refers to a cycle of seven cycles. This cycle is a week of cycles. In Scripture, seven usually speaks of levels of completeness or perfection.

It is also helpful to realize that cycles can be intertwined. It is impossible to calculate just how long the creative cycles of the first creative account were. Some of them could have even been overlapping cycles that are still in process. Ezekiel 1:16 refers to the overlapping aspect of cycles by speaking of wheels within wheels.

The first chapter in Genesis reveals God's full creative intention in a week of cycles. It focuses on the earth, its atmosphere, and life forms as the place God created to bring His offspring into reality. The forming and making details are not provided because this was a very short overview of a very large creative process.

The retelling in the second chapter begins to provide more detail of the sixth cycle of the creation week. It can appear we are still in the sixth cycle because God is still creating His host of offspring.

Another point can be made concerning "the man." The

Hebrew word *adam* is translated "Adam" 11 times in the first three chapters of Genesis and as "man" 15 times. The Old Testament continues to translate adam hundreds of times as man. The man noted in the first chapter and the Adam in the second chapter are not two different creations. The second account just elaborates and gives us details as it focuses on the sixth creative cycle and the process of making mankind.

The seventh verse of the second chapter proceeds to tell us how God made the first man. The process involved fusing properties from the natural and spiritual realms into a new life form.

> *The LORD God formed man of dust from the ground, and breathed into his nostrils the breath of life; and man became a living being* (Genesis 2:7).

After making one, God formed the one into two beings.

> *The LORD God fashioned into a woman the rib which He had taken from the man, and brought her to the man.* (Genesis 2:22).

This forming and making of the first man and woman set the stage for God to birth and form throughout history all the host of His offspring.

> *Now the man called his wife's name Eve, because she was the mother of all the living* (Genesis 3:20).

> *Now the man had relations with his wife Eve, and she conceived and gave birth to Cain, and she said, "I have gotten a manchild with the help of the LORD"* (Genesis 4:1).

The rest of Scripture records the ongoing process God is

using to birth, form, and reform the hosts that are noted in the first account of the creative week (see Genesis 2:1).

Each of our lives begins with a conception and subsequent forming in mother's womb. This is the first of many changes that accompany our ongoing growth and development.

The Changeless One created change. In time and space, creating involves multiple beginnings as well as forming and re-forming processes, to make and mold His will into a growing and developing reality. God creates and He makes!

Form and Mold

In 1902, Adelaide Pollard sat in a prayer meeting, discouraged because she had been unable to raise funds to go to Africa as a missionary. There she overheard an old woman pray, "It really doesn't matter what You do with us, Lord, just have Your own way with our lives."

Pollard, a hymn writer, was inspired by what the woman said and went home that night to write the following hymn. Perhaps you've sung it.

Have Thine own way, Lord! Have Thine own way!
  Thou art the Potter, I am the clay.
Mold me and make me after Thy will,
  While I am waiting, yielded and still.

Have Thine own way, Lord! Have Thine own way!
  Search me and try me, Master, today!
Whiter than snow, Lord, wash me just now,
  As in Thy presence humbly I bow.
Have Thine own way, Lord! Have Thine own way!

Wounded and weary, help me, I pray!
Power, all power, surely is Thine!
Touch me and heal me, Savior divine.

Have Thine own way, Lord! Have Thine own way!
Hold o'er my being absolute sway!
Fill with Thy Spirit 'till all shall see
Christ only, always, living in me. *(Public Domain)*

The prophet Isaiah wrote of the same sentiments.

> *But now, O LORD, You are our Father, we are the clay, and You our potter; and all of us are the work of Your hand* (Isaiah 64:8).

When the Changeless One sends His will into the earth, changes come to improve and enlarge what He has begun.

> *But one has testified somewhere, saying, "What is man, that You remember him...? You have made him for a little while lower than the angels; You have crowned him with glory and honor, and have appointed him over the works of Your hands; You have put all things in subjection under his feet...But now we do not yet see all things subjected to him"* (Hebrews 2:6-8).

God is not finished having offspring. He is not done molding us into His heart CAP, which is why we "do not yet see" a full reality. God is still birthing, forming, and molding His offspring into disciplined children.

What is it in us that reflects God as a mirror or resembles Him as a son? It is not how we physically look or dress, our male or female gender, the color of our flesh, or any genes from our natural heritage.

Peter speaks of the "qualities of the hidden person of the heart" (1 Peter 3:4). Our heart is what God is really interested in. It's the most moldable part of us.

> *For out of the heart come evil thoughts, murders...false witness, and slanders* (Matthew 15:19).

> *And He said to him, "You shall love the Lord your God with all your heart..."* (Matthew 22:37).

> *That He would grant you, according to the riches of His glory, to be strengthened with power through His Spirit in the inner man, so that Christ may dwell in your hearts* (Ephesians 3:16-17).

When we commune with God, our spirit connects to His Spirit, and we are strengthened by a certain dwelling of Christ in our heart. The depth of His dwelling dictates just how much He affects how we act and what we do. In the book *What Is Man?* we explain in-depth that the scriptural definition of heart is the expressive function of our being. Our heart is our moldable character, attitude, and personality (CAP).

- **Character** speaks of our moral fiber.

- **Attitude** refers to our temperament leanings.

- **Personality** speaks of our social behaviors.

The natural eye cannot see these features, but they are easily perceived by most people. We all begin our consciousness in this life, and we develop as we are able to perceive. We are learning to be children of God. How well does our expressive heart reflect and resemble our heavenly Father's heart?

The beginning of a created thing can appear to the undiscerning eye to be a finished work. We have learned that salvation, forgiveness, and repentance have beginnings that include follow-up processes. Everything God does in our life has beginnings that institute changes.

Jesus gave an example of this process in the parable of the seed. When God's word is sown in good soil (as in our heart), His word takes root to stabilize maturing growth. As growth occurs a fruitfulness results.

Now the parable is this: the seed is the word of God...But the seed in the good soil, these are the ones who have heard the word in an honest and good heart, and hold it fast, and bear fruit with perseverance (Luke 8:11, 15).

As we faithfully trust in God and commit ourselves to His relational ways in the culture of Christ, we can be sure that God will accomplish what He has begun.

For I am confident of this very thing, that He who began a good work in you will perfect it until the day of Christ Jesus (Philippians 1:6).

For it is God who is at work in you, both to will and to work for His good pleasure (Philippians 2:13).

The creative process, in our time and space environment, involves a forming, molding, and making before it becomes an established reality. So it is with our heart.

Transforming Growth

Smelting is the process by which pure metal is extracted from its ore in the refining fire of a super-heated furnace. Silver, tin, copper, and other metals are commonly refined through the smelting process.

Metal ores usually contain other elements such as oxygen, sulfur, and rock material, which must be removed to yield pure metal. Extreme heat and catalysts such as coal and limestone are added to break down the ore. In metallurgy, these catalysts are referred to as flux. They aid the release of gasses, slag, and rock gangue (the worthless parts of the ore), and render the metal more refined.

In the same way, the heat of life's trials and testing are meant to cleanse us of non-Christlike elements. These cleansings accelerate our growth into refined reflections and resemblances of God's heart character, attitude, and personality (CAP).

> *For He is like a refiner's fire and like fullers' soap. He will sit as a smelter and purifier of silver, and He will purify the sons of Levi and refine them like gold and silver, so that they may present to the Lord offerings in righteousness* (Malachi 3:2-3).

> *And to the eyes of the sons of Israel the appearance of the glory of the LORD was like a consuming fire on the mountain top* (Exodus 24:17).

> *For our God is a consuming fire* (Hebrews 12:29).

Yes, God is a consuming fire. But He only consumes the dross in us. No heat or refining action is meant to harm anyone. The smelting process is only intended to harm the dross and remove impurities—to clean us up.

It is the abundance of dross in our life that keeps us from

being very moldable in the Father's hand. Our growth into the Father's CAP requires us to let go of the impurities that keep us from becoming purer gold.

Our heavenly Father's love keeps Him seeking our good. He does not want to leave any of us in our impure or immature condition. Anytime we feel that the heat is turned up, it's because He is going after more dross. We need to learn to let it go of what was and keep grasping onto what is happening.

Fine gold can be molded into many beautiful expressions. Each time we endure cleansing activity, we become purer gold. The refining transforms us into better representatives of God's heart.

> *And do not be conformed to this world, but be transformed by the renewing of your mind, so that you may prove what the will of God is, that which is good and acceptable and perfect* (Romans 12:2).

God sees us from His eternal perspective as pure gold and refined silver. He looks beyond our dross and can see the Godlike CAP that is resident in us. It may be buried deep inside, but it is there. He lovingly refers to us as "the apple of His eye" (Zechariah 2:8).

We participants in the culture of Christ want God to have His way with us and to progressively do what is necessary to refine us. This is why we pray as the Psalmist did:

> *Wash me thoroughly from my iniquity and cleanse me from my sin...Purify me with hyssop, and I shall be clean; Wash me, and I shall be whiter than snow...Create in me a clean heart, O God, and renew a steadfast spirit within*

*me...Restore to me the joy of Your salvation and sustain
me with a willing spirit* (Psalm 51:2, 7, 10-12).

The Way of Salvation gives us an overview of the work God
is doing in our lives. The Way of Change helps us appreciate
our cleaning, smelting, molding, and growing developmental
changes. Our maturing growth depends a lot on our response
to God's cleansing work in us.

Rahab the harlot responded well and was blessed (see James
2:25). Michal was born a princess but despised God's work in
David and fell short (see 2 Samuel 6:20-23). Gideon felt in-
adequate but responded to God's call and became a mighty
deliverer (see Judges 6:7-8).

God's enabling grace will assist our CAP transformations
only to the extent that we allow Him. Let us become more
moldable and pliable in His hands.

More So Process

God designed life to assist our birth and development into
children who reflect and resemble His heart character, attitude, and personality (CAP). Growth requires that we be
flexible. We cannot remain as we were for growth requires
change. While God is at work in us, our agreement is a necessity. We must choose to be flexible enough to be molded.
Our cleansing level of maturity depends on it.

We can accept God's forgiveness and find some release from
our bondage. Then, as Israel of old, if we cease to submit to
God's work in us, we stay in our wilderness. Do we want to
continue to deal with the dross and impurities we inherited
from our captivity?

We all tend to learn the ways of man before we discover our need for the ways of God.

> *However, the spiritual is not first, but the natural; then the spiritual* (1 Corinthians 15:46).

Research shows that a new idea can battle old thought patterns for up to thirty days. Then, over the next three years, the brain creates new neural pathways to support the new thought. New perceptions take time to settle in.

When we turn to God, we invite God to transform our thoughts. This begins to form new neural pathways to support our new understandings. This is part of the process God uses to establish His ways in us. Stay in the process!

We should realize that while new perceptions are finding root in us, we will continue to be tempted by the old. Many impure thoughts, feelings, and attitudes that have held us captive can still show up. If we should turn away and quit affirming the new thoughts, the new neural pathways will stop developing. We could revert to past ideas and allow old destructive thought patterns to gain more than a foothold.

Scripture encourages us to actively reverse our trend toward anti-God thoughts, attitudes, and influences.

> *We are destroying speculations and every lofty thing raised up against the knowledge of God, and we are taking every thought captive to the obedience of Christ* (2 Corinthians 10:5).

Every new insight we receive from God must go through the process of becoming established in us.

We all respond to change in one of three ways:

1) We are dragged into it as we fight, kick, and scream.

2) We hesitantly accept it.

3) We gratefully anticipate its transforming adjustment.

We want to understand that each change in our developing CAP generally brings one thought, feeling, attitude, and action at a time.

Let's not be so set in our ways that we are not open to adjustment. Surely each of us can admit that we have areas in our CAP that need improvement.

God will lead and guide us into fuller maturity if we remain open to His voice, soft to His touch, and flexible in His hand. The following verse is an important fact. After we put on the new self, we are still in need of renewing:

> *Do not lie to one another, since you laid aside the old self with its evil practices, and have put on the new self who is being renewed to a true knowledge according to the image of the One who created him* (Colossians 3:9-10).

We are never finished. As we improve in one area, God will shift our focus onto another that needs adjustment. He may help us change a strong tendency toward anger in one season and then deal with an inclination toward fear in another.

Just like the pear tree illustrated in the beginning of this chapter, our life is full of changing seasons. We may appear to be in a fruitful fall and then experience a winter season. God uses change to help us grow.

In this life, no one will fully understand, be wholly sinless, entirely holy, totally saved, or completely mature. Every growth change we experience requires testing and proving to become established.

Yes, God can and occasionally does interject a miraculous solution into our experience. We should recognize, however, that every immediate answer is only established through good follow-up.

Paul, in his later years, admitted he was still lacking and pressing on. Change was the order of his day.

> *Brethren, I do not regard myself as having laid hold of it yet; but one thing I do: forgetting what lies behind and reaching forward to what lies ahead, I press on toward the goal for the prize of the upward call of God in Christ Jesus* (Philippians 3:13-14).

Don't ever entertain discouragement. We will make it if we remain soft and stay flexible and adjustable. We are all offspring of God. Our response to His leading, as learning children, will insure His work in us continues.

> *For I am confident of this very thing, that He who began a good work in you will perfect it until the day* [time] *of Christ Jesus* (Philippians 1:6).

> *And so, those who have been chosen by God, holy and beloved, put on a heart of compassion, kindness, humility, gentleness, and patience* (Colossians 3:12).

Paul identifies in this verse several heart qualities that reflect and resemble God's character, attitude, and personality. We should put on these qualities until they are fully established in us, as they are in Christ.

God is patient with us and we need to be patient with each

other. Let's keep the larger picture in mind and not be overwhelmed by current situations. Remember, others are in stages of change as well.

God is the same yesterday, today, and forever. He never changes, but we must. God not only creates us, He desires to empower our forming growth and remold us from the inside out. In the culture of Christ we progressively grow into people who reflect and resemble His heart attitude. Our growth processes are easier when we embrace improving change.

We do not want to be satisfied with the fringe benefits of God's grace and mercy but seek to be conformed to the fullness of Christ. Sincere repentance brings us into change. The changes we experience help us learn to be adjustable.

As we yield to the Smelter's cleansing and the Potter's reforming, we become better reflections and resemblances of God's heart. Stay soft and be flexible.

Memorize:

God can turn my mess into a message and my test into a testimony.

Questions to Consider:

1. What is your response to change and variables?

2. What happens when we quit changing and adjusting?

3. What attitudes are projected when we assume we are done growing?

Chapter 6

The Way of Balance Strengthens Us

A man was having a conversation with the Lord one day and said, "Lord, I would like to know what heaven is like."

The Lord then led him to two doors. He opened one of the doors and the man looked in. In the middle of the room was a large table. In the middle of the table was a large pot of stew, which smelled delicious and made the man's mouth water.

The people sitting around the table were thin and sickly. They appeared to be famished. They were holding spoons with very long handles that were strapped to their arms. Each found it possible to reach into the pot of stew and take a spoonful, but because the handle was longer than their arms, they could not get the spoons back into their mouths. The man shuddered at the sight of their misery and suffering.

The Lord said, "You have seen hell."

They went to the next room and opened the door. It was exactly the same as the first one. There was the large round table with the large pot of stew, which made the man's mouth water. The people were equipped with the same long handled spoons, but here the people were plump and well nourished, laughing and talking.

The man said, "I don't understand."

"It is simple," said the Lord, "it requires but one skill. You see, these have learned to feed each other, while the greedy only think of themselves."

This story demonstrates the Way of Balance because the healthy way to live includes a care for "me, myself, and I" that is balanced by a care for others. A willingness to share with one another is a demonstration of balance.

We have come to understand that our heavenly Father designed life to be a process for birthing and initially developing offspring into His heart character, attitude, and personality (CAP).

We have seen that our sincere repentance brings us into a change process that invites God's graceful assistance. Our repentant adjustments teach us to be more flexible.

In the Way of Balance, we realize our flexibility can lift us into a grander truth and reality than what we might know and experience in the twisted world of division.

Godly Value

Balance is usually described as the cancellation of all forces by equal and opposing forces. In the context of our study, balance does not cancel opposing forces; it receives value from each side without fully committing to one or the other side.

Positive and negative forces provide an example. We all relate to positive as a preferred value, and we try to avoid negativity. Balance however, appreciates the value in each and then demonstrates a greater value. It is a position that dwells amid differences between opposing forces. Balance relates to the value in these differences as contributing factors.

A higher truth is often observed when examining issues with a balanced perspective than any opposing side of an issue can provide. Balance is a major ingredient in sharing ideas because it depends on the activity of giving and receiving of what might be considered conflicting values.

Scripture tells us that God made the natural universe and all things in it. So something of God must dwell in and through everything in the natural realm.

> *For from Him and through Him and to Him are all things. To Him be the glory forever* (Romans 11:36).

> *There is…one Lord, one faith, one baptism, one God and Father of all who is over all and through all and in all* (Ephesians 4:4-6).

> *He is before all things, and in Him all things hold together* (Colossians 1: 17).

The natural creation is held together by a force that flows from its Creator. This force can be likened to the connective value of balance. While each part of the creation has its distinct differences, they are all held together as a contributing member of the larger picture.

Everything in the natural realm illustrates balance as each one gives and receives support. The four climate seasons are very different, yet they are needed support systems. Spring needs the dormancy of winter and summer requires a spring. To the undiscerning eye, nature's ecosystems can appear as separate functions, but in reality, each supports the other. When one is interrupted, the others are affected.

The spirit of life in each of us comes from our heavenly Father. As individuals, we are bits, pieces, and portions of His divine reality. Just as God shares something of His essence (Spirit) with us and we share with Him, we need to learn how to share life with one another.

> *If we love one another, God abides in us, and His love is perfected in us* (1 John 4:12).

> *We ought always to give thanks to God for you...because your faith is greatly enlarged, and the love of each one of you toward one another grows ever greater* (2 Thessalonians 1:3).

The relational love that flows from God binds us to Him and to one another. This love demonstrates balance as a give and take value. While each part of the creation has its distinct differences, they are all held together by a value that emanates from their Creator. Balance is of God.

Our active involvement in the culture of Christ compels us to be sharing people. God, in the culture of Christ, draws us into greater relational heights when we are supporting one another. By the way, balance will not give away everything so we have nothing more to share.

Life always works best when we live the way we are designed to function, as complements. When we view our differences as complements, we all become better people. God created His first human offspring by making one and then separating the one into two. This was so each one would know life as a support alongside one another.

> *So the LORD God caused a deep sleep to fall upon the man, and he slept; then He took one of his ribs and closed up the flesh...The LORD God fashioned into a woman the rib which He had taken from the man, and brought her to the man* (Genesis 2:19-22).

Adam and Eve were wonderful creations separately. However, God designed them to work together as a harmonious team. As complements, they were able to exceed their individuality and experience balance.

This principle was further illustrated in the Garden of Eden. God planted two trees in the midst of the Garden: the tree of life and the tree of the knowledge of good and evil. Both trees were to play complementary roles in His plan to birth and grow children. God said all the trees were good for food.

> *Out of the ground the LORD God caused to grow every tree that is pleasing to the sight and good for food; the tree of life in the midst of the garden, and the tree of the knowledge of good and evil* (Genesis 2:9).

Since life was designed to be a developing growth process, God activated their ability to choose by giving them a choice.

> *But from the tree of the knowledge of good and evil you shall not eat, for in the day that you eat from it you will surely die* (Genesis 2:17).

The sin in the Garden had little to do with what they ate or did. The original sin was their decision to ignore God and live independent of His guidance.

> *When the woman saw that the tree was good for food, and that it was a delight to the eyes, and that the tree was desirable to make one wise, she took from its fruit and ate; and she gave also to her husband with her, and he ate* (Genesis 3:6).

Adam and Eve chose to follow an influence that sought to separate them from God's guidance. Their choice to submit and ignore God's complementary approach to life complicated their clarity regarding the godly value in complementary relationships.

Guiding Perspective

Instead of seeing one another as complements, they began to see each other as contrasts. This deception skewed their understanding and resulted in division. When Adam and Eve lost sight of godly balance, life really did get complicated.

"Me, myself, and I" became more important than "us." A *me* versus *you* contrast skewed their ability to view their differences as contributing values. Complementing "ANDs" became contrasting "ORs." You *and* I became you *or* I.

Their newly acquired god-complex caused them to become cautious of differences. Individuals began to be viewed with suspicion. As their complementary perspective took a back seat, they began to hold each other in mistrust.

The deception also introduced them to fear and shame. They began to cover up in each other's presence and sharing became a guarded activity. When God came to visit with them, they hid from His presence.

They heard the sound of the LORD God walking in the garden in the cool of the day, and the man and his wife hid themselves from the presence of the LORD God among the trees of the garden (Genesis 3:8).

Their newly acquired mistrust of God clouded their ability to be open and honest. Instead of repenting and submitting to the Father's mercy, they shifted blame and made excuses. Adam blamed both God and Eve, the only "others" that were available.

The man said, "The woman whom You gave to be with me, she gave me from the tree, and I ate" (Genesis 3:12).

It is interesting to see how a god-complex does not work very well in God's presence. Adam's new "I'll decide for myself" attitude found no secure ground to stand on. Their corrupted god-complex caused them to think they were sufficient in and of themselves. God even said they were now as "one of Us." They were no longer able to receive what God wanted to share.

The LORD God said, "Behold, the man has become like one of Us"...therefore the LORD God sent him out from the garden of Eden, to cultivate the ground from which he was taken (Genesis 3:22-23).

As an act of mercy, God removed them from the Garden lest they eat of the tree of life and remain unrepentant forever. God would let them live with the independence they had chosen, until they would choose to die to their god-complex and be more open to receive from Him and one another.

We are all given free will and its ability to choose. Yes, God allows us to choose wrongly. Life is designed to provide us with a choice. When we choose unwisely, we can repent and God will help us correct. Without a repentant willingness to change, we continue in our suffering longer than we should.

And so it continues. We begin life as a baby, wanting what we want, insisting our need is more important that anyone's. As we receive what we need, we learn either to be a thankful person or a demanding person with a strengthened god-complex.

God made the one and then re-formed the one into two, so we could be sharing complements. Our individuality is not a bad thing if we are not so self-centered that we become selfish and unbalanced.

When God delivered Israel out of Egypt, His guiding presence came to instruct them. Just like our first parents, Adam and Eve, Israel was suspect and untrusting of His presence.

> *Then they said to Moses, "Speak to us yourself and we will listen; but let not God speak to us, or we will die"* (Exodus 20:19).

Israel rejected the presence of God among them and chose Moses to be a go-between. They were unwilling to accept the presence of God with them as a value that would lift them into a more balanced life experience. As a result, God gave them a coded Law as a temporary fix until they would desire and accept His guiding presence among them.

> *But before faith came, we were kept in custody under the law, being shut up to the faith which was later to be re-*

vealed. Therefore the Law has become our tutor to lead us to Christ, so that we may be justified by faith (Galatians 3:23-24).

See Appendix VI: Separating Influence

The Law remains a primary guide to lift our perceptions higher until we personally accept God into our life experience. God, in the culture of Christ, comes to help us all become people who are more balanced so our personal importance does not outweigh our desire to contribute.

> *Behold, the virgin shall be with child and shall bear a son, and they shall call his name Immanuel, which translated means, "God with us"* (Matthew 1:23).

> *And the Word became flesh, and dwelt among us, and we saw His glory, glory as of the only begotten from the Father, full of grace and truth* (John 1:14).

> *Go therefore and make disciples...and lo, I am with you always, even to the end of the age* (Matthew 28:19-20).

As in the verses above, God wants to be "with us" and "among us" as a balance influence throughout our life journey.

A divisionary attitude wants to continue its influence over us. It wants to remain in our midst as a divisive perspective and keep strife stirred up among us. Imbalance, caused by this dividing attitude, keeps us in deception and pointing our finger at each other. A contrast oriented perspective loves the phrase "no compromise." Its divisive attitude keeps stunting our growth into God's reflection and resemblance.

On the other hand, a separation oriented attitude helps us attain and maintain a balanced give and take approach toward each other and facilitates our growth and development. We want to be balanced people who seek to give and receive as complements.

God wants to be our guiding light—the primary influence in our midst, among us, and in our sharing of life.

Flexible Adjustments

During my teenage and early adult years, I traveled the country with my parents. While Dad and Mom had a message to share, we were also inclined to examine what other people believed and consider insight that we had not yet seen.

Many times we moved into an area for a few weeks and sometimes for months. I was exposed to many ministries and a variety of messages. We considered what was said and judged its veracity, whether it was something we would embrace or reject.

I listened and read the materials. When I saw a teaching that enlarged my understanding and love of God, I would accept elements of it and adjust my personal belief system. Sometimes I had to dismiss elements of what I previously understood that no longer fit into my developing perspective. I learned to adjust.

Webster defines dogmatism as: "stubborn or intolerant adherence to one's opinions or prejudices." A dogmatic person will misinterpret evidence to support a position. For example, for centuries, scientists believed that the universe was created to operate in a totally ordered and predictable fashion. Some, like Newton, even likened its operation to a clock. This guided scientific thought for many generations.

In the mid-twentieth century, another theory emerged: the chaos theory. It states that absolute predictability is impossible. Instead, we should deal in probabilities. This was a massive paradigm shift in scientific theory.

The ways of God teach us that our real stability is not in any rigid ability to maintain dogmatic positions but rather in our ability to be teachable and to adjust.

We want to understand that balance is nothing like compromise. Compromise gives up something of value for peace while it maintains a contrast either/or position. Balance, on the other hand, is an attitude we maintain so we can recognize and partake of reasonable complements. We accept what harmonizes and dismiss what does not. When we see our differences as possible complements, something constructive is able to happen.

Consider airplane parts. On their own they would fall to the ground, but together they can produce flight. Each part contains something to contribute. It is the same with lamp parts. Together, plugged into an energy source, they can produce light.

When we come together as complements, something of greater value can be produced. For example, a symphony orchestra arranges many instruments into harmonization to produce a more beautiful array of sounds.

A lion is strong, aggressive, tough, and self-assured. A lamb, on the other hand, is fragile, passive, tender, and vulnerable.

While these are contrasting values, Scripture portrays Jesus Christ as one with the qualities of both a lion and a lamb:

> *And one of the elders said to me, "Stop weeping; behold, the Lion that is from the tribe of Judah, the Root of David, has overcome" ...When He had taken the book, the four living creatures and the twenty-four elders fell down before the Lamb* (Revelation 5:5, 8).

In Christ, the Lion's strength is tempered with the Lamb's tenderness. This is another good visual of balance.

A perspective based on balance helps us learn to adjust and gravitate toward greater truths, unlike separating perspectives, which hinder our appreciation of a grander perspective. There are many factors that hinder our ability to see differences as complements. We can be restricted by an accepted belief system, an unforgiving attitude, self-condemnation, ethnic heritage, or even by the seasons of life.

Our ability to experience balance can also be severely limited if we are not willing to admit we could be wrong or if we are not open to repentant change.

> *Give instruction to a wise man and he will be still wiser, teach a righteous man and he will increase his learning* (Proverbs 9:9).

Scripture encourages us to be strong in the Lord and to let His strength be perfected in our adjusting flaws.

> *And He has said to me, "My grace is sufficient for you, for power is perfected in weakness." Most gladly, therefore, I will rather boast about my weaknesses, so that the power of Christ may dwell in me* (2 Corinthians 12:9).

When we maintain flexible adaptability, we are more likely to experience an adjusting balance. Balance is where the Prince of Peace reigns, leads, and guides.

> *For He Himself is our peace, who made both groups into one and broke down the barrier of the dividing wall...so that in Himself He might make the two into one new man, thus establishing peace, and might reconcile them both in one body to God through the cross, by it having put to death the enmity* (Ephesians 2:14-16).

The one new man is a combination of many contributing members, along with several thought patterns and beliefs systems.

Balance is not a value that can be understood by looking at one side of an issue, argument, or conflict. Balance can only be appreciated when each side is examined for complementary values and are allowed to contribute to an understanding of the big picture.

When we open ourselves to balance, we can focus on the complementary values that exist in each other's differences. We are able to recognize mutual values in people, heritages, ideas, and even beliefs. Greater truths dwell beyond the partial understanding of where we are currently at in our walk. When we are flexible and embrace a balanced perspective that dwells above separating division, our lives are strengthened and stabilized.

A balanced perspective allows us to ponder ideas and interact with one another in a more loving way. An attitude of balance keeps us positioned to receive the insight that God may yet want to reveal. When what may appear to be a contrast is allowed to complement, everyone tends to benefit.

God designed our life on earth to be a give and take experience so we would grow into His intention. When we allow God to contribute to our lives and share with each other, everyone benefits.

Peaceful Strength

A balanced perspective can also help us appropriately live this life as natural and spiritual beings. Our life in the earth includes our body, soul, and spirit. Thus we are designed to partake of both the natural and spiritual realms at the same time in a dynamic balance.

God created, supports, stabilizes, and holds all things in a complementary balance. We become more godly when we approach situations and one another with an also/and attitude. When we see primarily with a balanced eye, we can approach each other with a view to be complementary.

We want to recognize that most sides of an issue contain value. When we see things as contrasts, we tend to settle on one side of various issues and say, "It is either my way or the highway." Balance helps us discern possible complements.

An old fashioned teeter-totter or balance board demonstrates the need to make adjustments to find and maintain balance. Once a balance point is found, we can then shift on the device to stay in balance. Balance is also illustrated by riding a bike, skiing, or surfing. To maintain upright forward movement, a rider must constantly make adjustments as conditions change.

Along life's way, we want to be flexible enough to make adjustments to maintain a good balance. This is a more godly attitude than a distorted god-complex provides.

Finding balance in life is a stabilizing influence in all of our thoughts, ideologies, and relationships. It can facilitate greater understanding and more meaningful interactions. Approaching situations with balance can defuse arguments, encourage the dejected, and restore broken relationships.

Balance can also be demonstrated in our approach toward Scripture. We can view truths as contradictory doctrines, or we can view them as complements that support a greater understanding. A greater truth resides in a balanced approach to any Scripture. The following two versions of one verse illustrate how we can view what is said in two different ways:

Jesus said to him, "I am the way, and the truth, and the life; no one comes to the Father but through Me" (John 14:6).

Jesus says to him, "I am the truthful way to live; the only way to know God as Father is to approach Him as a son" (John 14:6, Christ Culture paraphrase).

Greek scholars verify this verse can be translated both ways. When we combine what can appear as different values, this verse provides a simple clarity that we can all understand and easily promote.

Jesus declared the Good News that we are born into life to submissively share our life with God and one another. We are made to complement our heavenly Father as children and to complement one another as siblings. The Way of Balance shows us how to continue our salvation journey under the peaceful reign of God's influence:

For the kingdom of God is not eating and drinking, but righteousness and peace and joy in the Holy Spirit (Romans 14:17).

We experience the kingdom of God when we respond to the Father's governing guidance. Offspring become children of God and together we are the body of Christ in the earth. Submissive children are taught by our heavenly Father and learn to lovingly share with one another.

But speaking the truth in love, we are to grow up in all aspects into Him who is the head, even Christ, from whom the whole body, being fitted and held together by what every joint supplies, according to the proper working of each individual part, causes the growth of the body for the building up of itself in love (Ephesians 4:15-16).

In the culture of Christ we are in the process of adjusting and becoming more balanced people. Balanced children can represent and share our Father's love more appropriately. As is illustrated in our opening story of heaven and hell, a balanced perspective keeps us from spiritual malnutrition.

The Father wants to be our guiding influence through life:

"But this is the covenant which I will make..." declares the Lord, "I will put My law within them and on their heart I will write it; and I will be their God, and they shall be My people" (Jeremiah 31:33).

As we experience the ways of God, we learn to view one another and different thoughts as possible complements.

...until we all attain to the unity of the faith, and of the knowledge of the Son of God, to a mature man, to the

measure of the stature which belongs to the fullness of Christ (Ephesians 4:13).

Let us subscribe to balanced thinking and living. It will help us understand better, maintain a peaceable spirit, and develop an attitude that is less judgmental.

We can rise into God's perspective and experience the strength of dynamic balance. Godly balance will bring us into a strength and stability not found anywhere else. Yes, we can maintain a repentant attitude, a forgiving heart, and be open to improving change.

Greater truth exists beyond the partial understanding that resides in our separations. The Prince of Peace reigns in the balance that exists on a plane above contrasts. The ways of God in the culture of Christ help us become flexible, embrace balance, and know stabilizing strength.

The Way of Balance reveals how we can better reflect and resemble the heart character, attitude, and personality (CAP) of our heavenly Father. Each of the ways of God help us live a fuller life in the world.

Memorize:

"God grant me the grace to accept the things I cannot change, the courage to change the things I can, and the wisdom to know the difference" (Reinhold Niebuhr).

Questions to Consider:

1. Why is balance different than compromise?

2. What are some of the different life roles and seasons that can affect our balance?

3. Identify examples 1) where a balanced approach has created a greater experience in your life and 2) where a divisive approach has produced pain and suffering.

Chapter 7

The Way of Interaction Matures Us

One day a teacher asked her students to list the names of the other students in the room on two sheets of paper, leaving a space between each name. Then she told them to think of the nicest thing they could say about each of their classmates and write it down.

It took the remainder of the class period to finish their assignment. As the students left the room, each one handed in their paper.

That Saturday, the teacher wrote down the name of each student on a separate sheet of paper and listed what everyone else had said about that individual. On Monday she gave each student his or her list. Before long, the entire class was smiling.

"Really?" she heard whispered. "I never knew that I meant anything to anyone!" and, "I didn't know others liked me so much." These were typical of the comments.

No one ever mentioned those papers in class again. She never knew if they discussed them after class or with their parents. It didn't matter, the exercise had accomplished its purpose. The students remained happy with themselves and one another. That group moved on.

Several years later, one of the students was killed in Vietnam and his teacher attended the funeral of that special student. She had never seen a serviceman in a military coffin before. He looked so handsome, mature.

The church was packed with his friends. One by one those who loved him took a last walk by the coffin. The teacher was the last one to pass the coffin. As she stood there, one of the soldiers who acted as a pallbearer came up to her.

"Were you Mark's math teacher?" he asked.

She nodded, "Yes."

Then he said, "Mark talked about you a lot."

After the funeral, most of Mark's former classmates went together to a luncheon. Mark's mother and father were there, obviously waiting to speak with his teacher.

"We want to show you something," his father said, taking a wallet out of his pocket. "They found this on Mark when he was killed. We thought you might recognize it."

Opening the billfold, he carefully removed two worn pieces of notebook paper that had obviously been taped, folded, and refolded many times. The teacher knew without looking that the pieces of paper were the ones on which she had listed all the good things each of Mark's classmates had said about him.

"Thank you so much for doing that," Mark's mother said. "As you can see, Mark treasured it."

All of Mark's former classmates started to gather around. Charlie smiled rather sheepishly and said, "I still have my list. It's in the top drawer of my desk at home." His wife said, "Charlie asked me to put his in our wedding album."

"I have mine too," Marilyn said. "It's in my diary." Then Vicki, another classmate, reached into her purse and showed her frazzled list to the group. "I carry this with me all the time," and without batting an eyelash, she continued: "I think we all saved our lists."

It is important to tell people they are special and are valued. Our supportive interaction with one another has many enduring effects.

The Apostle Paul's writings continually instruct us to encourage, strengthen, and build one another up.

> *Therefore encourage one another and build up one another, just as you also are doing* (1 Thessalonians 5:11).

Interaction is the give and take activity we experience when we relate with others. Our interaction involves relational contact and sharing communication. While interaction is not a biblical word, it is a scriptural concept and a necessary activity in achieving any balance. Interaction is a primary catalyst in all our relationships with God and with each other.

Relational Intent

The first two chapters of Genesis provide references to God's relational intention for mankind—for each of us.

God created man in His own image, in the image of God He created him; male and female He created them (Genesis 1:27).

Then the LORD God said, "It is not good for the man to be alone; I will make him a helper suitable for him" (Genesis 2:18).

The LORD God commanded the man, saying, "From any tree of the garden you may eat freely; but from the tree of the knowledge of good and evil you shall not eat, for in the day that you eat from it you will surely die" (Genesis 2:16-17).

See the clues? Being alone and separated is not good. God created *him* to be *them*. He gave them license to partake of the many trees, and they were to leave the one alone. We are relational beings that are intended for interaction.

When Adam and Eve ignored God's instruction and chose the one, their perceptions changed. "Me, myself and I" became more important than "we, us, and our." In their mind, all complements began to appear as contrasts. When we ignore God and His ways, our counterparts appear as competitors. This hinders encouraging and maturing interaction.

Although they ignored God and turned from His guidance, He still came to interact and commune with them. Yes, He knew what they had done, but He still cared about their well-being and gave them the opportunity to repent. Since repentance did not happen, God removed them from the Garden. As the best of fathers, God knew it would be detrimental to their growth if they partook of the Tree of Life and remained unrepentant.

God then invited Adam's sons into fellowship. While Abel

made efforts to properly relate and interact, Cain followed Adam's error and went further away from God. He rejected God's guidance, got angry with God, and killed Abel. He then left the presence of God to live in the land of Nod.

Then Cain went out from the presence of the Lord, and settled in the land of Nod, east of Eden (Genesis 4:16).

The Hebrew word translated "Nod" means vagrancy (unsettled; without peace, stability, or direction). Cain chose to ignore God's interactive fellowship and left the presence of God to dwell as an unstable vagrant. Life without God produces the "Nod Effect."

Jesus illustrated humanity's independence in the story of the Prodigal Son. The Prodigal left his father's influence, did his own thing, made unwise decisions, and wound up living by himself in a pigpen (the Nod Effect). We are told that when the Prodigal's senses cleared, he returned to his father's forgiveness and loving care.

And not many days later, the younger son gathered everything together and...squandered his estate with loose living....But when he came to his senses...he got up and came to his father...And the son said to him, "Father, I have sinned against heaven and in your sight..." The father said... "This son of mine was dead and has come to life again; he was lost and has been found" (Luke 15:11-24).

Interactive fellowship with our heavenly Father allows us to receive His perspective about life and His direction for our life's purpose. This is how we learn to live as Spirit-led people.

With Us, Among Us, in Our Midst

Throughout human history, God has sought to be a major influence in our lives. He began with our first parents Adam and Eve, and then their first offspring, Cain and Abel. While we don't know how many responded to God's call for fellowship, Scripture tells us of some who did. Enoch lived in the seventh generation after Adam and after becoming a father; he responded and experienced life with God.

> *Then Enoch walked with God three hundred years after he became the father of Methuselah, and he had other sons and daughters...and he was not, for God took him* (Genesis 5:22, 25).

> *Enoch was taken up so that he would not see death; and he was not found because God took him up; for...he was pleasing to God* (Hebrews 11:5).

We are told of Noah experiencing the grace of God that helped him survive the flood, which destroyed the wicked people of his day. We read of Abraham responding and interacting with God as a friend.

> *And Abraham believed God, and it was reckoned to him as righteousness, and he was called the friend of God* (James 2:23).

Abraham's offspring came to be known as the people of Israel. During their 1500 year Old Testament history, many experienced personal fellowship with God. King David reported in his writings that the majority of the people of Israel only *knew about* God's miraculous interventions. Moses, however, *interacted* with God and began to *understand* His ways and methods among us.

He made known His ways to Moses, His acts to the sons of Israel (Psalms 103:7).

While Moses did not physically enter into the promise land, he responded to God's invitation to interact and communicated with Him as a friend. As a result, Moses became an outstanding expression of godliness in his day.

When the Old Testament account concluded, the majority of the people's response to God was no more than religious exercises. Systematic religion is not a bad thing because it can facilitate our growth if we do not become satisfied and stop pursuing maturing interaction.

God invites us to seek Him—beyond the miracles, even beyond serving and working for Him. Like Moses, we can experience an interactive fellowship with God.

God began to intervene on our behalf in a more visual way when Jesus Christ appeared in history. God's desire to dwell with us, among us, and in our midst was demonstrated in the life of Christ.

And the Word became flesh, and dwelt among us (John 1:14).

And they shall call his name Immanuel, which translated means, "GOD WITH US" (Matthew 1:13).

What was from the beginning...we have seen and testify...indeed our fellowship is with the Father, and with His Son Jesus Christ (1 John 1:1-3).

God went the extra mile to clarify His desire to be involved in our lives. We are all intended to partake of His guiding presence, "whosoever will" may come.

Come to Me, all who are weary and heavy-laden, and I will give you rest (Matthew 11:28).

Jesus stood and cried out, saying, "If anyone is thirsty, let him come to Me and drink" (John 7:37)

For God so loved the world, that He gave His only begotten Son, that whoever believes in Him shall not perish, but have eternal life (John 3:16).

Both the Old and New Testaments tell us that God desires to dwell with us, among us, and in our midst.

I will dwell among the sons of Israel and will be their God (Exodus 29:45).

Be sure that it is those who are of faith who are sons of Abraham. And if you belong to Christ, then you are Abraham's descendants (Galatians 3:7, 29).

Go therefore and make disciples...and lo, I am with you always, even to the end... (Matthew 28:19-20).

...For He Himself [Jesus] *has said, "I will never desert you, nor will I ever forsake you"* (Hebrews 13:5).

After Jesus left the earth's time and space life, God sent His Holy Spirit to be His guiding presence. Thus, He would dwell with us, among us, and be in our midst. God has promised to be with each of us, if we will have Him. As people in that generation witnessed Christ among us, they responded to the presence of God in droves.

These men who have upset the world have come here also (Acts 17:6).

Recorded history tells us the Gospel of this culture had an overriding effect on most of the civilized world, so much so that in 318 AD the Roman emperor declared it to be the sanctioned faith of the empire.

Interactive Presence

Engineers tell us that twisted or braided rope composed of three strands is stronger than three individual strands of the same type of material. Why is this? It has to do with physics. When stress is put on an individual strand (such as when lifting or pulling a load), tears can develop down the length and circumference of the strand. However, when three strands are twisted or braided together, the tears would all have to occur at the same time and in the same location for the rope to fail.

We can compare a three-fold cord to the relationship between two people and the Lord. When God is part of the "cord," an additional unifying and strengthening power is added to the relationship.

Jesus told us the Scripture's primary purpose is to help us learn to interact with God and one another.

And He said to him, "'You shall love the Lord your God with all your heart, and with all your soul, and with all your mind.' This is the great and foremost commandment. The second is like it, 'You shall love your neighbor as yourself.' On these two commandments depend the whole Law and the Prophets" (Matthew 22:37-40).

When this was written, "The Law and Prophets" was a term that referred to all recorded Scripture. Jesus reduced all

Scripture into a simple dual relational concept: Love God completely and love one another respectfully. When we interact with God as our loving Father and relate to one another as siblings, we experience a strength that is illustrated by the three strand cord.

Scripture records for us the good, the bad, and the ugly of interaction. We can observe relational interactions and realize what works and what does not work. When our interactions with one another invite God's presence and include His insight, we are better able to reflect and resemble His heart:

> *For where two or three have gathered together in My name, I am there in their midst* (Matthew 18:20).

> *And let us consider how to stimulate one another to love and good deeds...encouraging one another; and all the more as you see the day drawing near* (Hebrews 10:24-25).

Scripture refers to God's presence among us with several terms: Israel, Church, children of God, sons of God, body of Christ, holy nation, royal priesthood, temple, and Kingdom of God. These names are not different groups. They are various functions within the Culture.

When we respond to God as His offspring, we function as children and sons of God. When we support one another, we function as the Church and body of Christ. When we worship, we are the Temple and function as a royal priesthood. And when we share light with others, we function as Israel and the Kingdom of God.

But to each one of us grace was given according to the measure of Christ's gift...for the equipping of the saints for the work of service, to the building up of the body of Christ (Ephesians 4:7, 12).

...until we all attain to the unity of the faith, and of the knowledge of the Son of God, to a mature man, to the measure of the stature which belongs to the fullness of Christ (Ephesians 4:13).

...from whom the whole body, being fitted and held together by what every joint supplies, according to the proper working of each individual part, causes the growth of the body for the building up of itself in love (Ephesians 4:16).

The New Testament addresses the issue of our godly interaction with one another over 70 times. Here are a few examples:

But if we walk in the Light as He Himself is in the Light, we have fellowship with one another (1 John 1:7).

Let no one seek his own good, but that of his neighbor (1 Corinthians 10:24).

...so that there may be no division in the body, but that the members may have the same care for one another (1 Corinthians 12:25).

This is My commandment, that you love one another, just as I have loved you. Greater love has no one than this, that one lay down his life for his friends (John 15:12-13).

These verses state that our interaction should resemble the loving life of Jesus Christ. We want to be fully committed to walking in the light of Christ that is experienced in the culture of Christ.

See Appendix VII: One Another

Scripture also says we are co-laborers with God and our interaction with each other is to be as members.

> *For we are God's fellow workers; you are God's field, God's building* (1 Corinthians 3:9).

We co-labor with God in three distinct ways:

1. God brings His offspring into existence through our marriage relationships.

2. We are involved in raising them into levels of maturity.

3. Our interaction as parents, family, friends, neighbors and coworkers contribute to each other's well-being and growing development.

Our appropriate interaction benefits everyone. Let's take a moment to read Isaiah 58:6-12 and notice how our godly interaction in the culture of Christ has a heavenly effect.

> *Is this not the fast which I choose, to loosen the bonds of wickedness...? Is it not to divide your bread with the hungry and bring the homeless poor into the house; when you see the naked, to cover him...?*
>
> *Then your light will break out like the dawn, and your recovery will speedily spring forth; and your righteousness will go before you...You will call, and the LORD will answer; you will cry, and He will say, "Here I am."*

If you remove the yoke from your midst, the pointing of the finger and speaking wickedness, and if you give yourself to the hungry...Then your light will rise in darkness...And the LORD will continually guide you, and satisfy your desire in scorched places, and give strength to your bones; and you will be like a watered garden, and like a spring of water whose waters do not fail (Isaiah 58:6-12).

The "fast" in this text speaks of our effort to devote time and energy to a spiritual or religious activity. God directs us in this passage to be helpful as interactive people.

Maturing Value

Scientific studies have proven the value of interaction. They reveal that we retain 10% of what we read, 20% of what we hear, 30% of what we see, and 50% of what we see *and* hear. However, we absorb and retain much more of what we read, hear, or see when we interact and express our thoughts, ideas, and insights. It is reported that we retain 70% of what we discuss. Our godly interaction is important.

This enhancing effect is demonstrated in ordinary foods like olives, grains, and grapes. The interactive process increases the value of each item. When olives are interacted upon, they become oil. Grains become bread. Grapes become wine.

Each of these transformations demonstrates the increased blessings that result from appropriate interaction. When we actively interact with God and with one another, it enriches everyone's life. This includes those who are being acted upon, we ourselves, and anyone observing.

The added benefits of interaction are also apparent when we interact as a team. One member can provide strength at the point of another's weakness. When diverse talents interact as complements the full team is benefited.

> *Two are better than one because they have a good return for their labor. For, if either of them falls, the one will lift up his companion. But woe to the one who falls when there is not another to lift him up…if one can overpower him who is alone, two can resist him. A cord of three strands is not quickly torn apart* (Ecclesiastes 4:9-10, 12).

When a crippled person and a blind person meet, they could say to each other, "We are handicapped" and go their separate ways. Or they can realize that if they function as complements, both will be helped. The crippled person's ability to see can give direction while the blind one provides mobility.

One person's area of strength can make up for another's weakness when we humbly interact with those equipped and gifted with the abilities we lack. Interaction can help bring all participants into a more mature state of balance.

Our proper interaction with God and with each other brings us into levels of maturity that are unavailable to us as individuals. We want to give ourselves to improving our communication skills.

Scripture describes godly maturity in different ways. Jesus referred to levels of maturity when He spoke of His disciples becoming friends and not just servants:

116

You are My friends if you do what I command you. No longer do I call you slaves, for the slave does not know what his master is doing; but I have called you friends, for all things that I have heard from My Father I have made known to you (John 15:14-15).

Jesus also said people will know we are His disciples by our interactive love. Disciples are children who are experiencing fellowship with our heavenly Father in the culture of Christ:

A new commandment I give to you, that you love one another, even as I have loved you, that you also love one another. By this all men will know that you are My disciples, if you have love for one another (John 13:34-35).

Our lack of interaction may be why some of us remain so immature. Our inability or unwillingness to interact with others keeps us from appropriate maturing growth.

...always learning and never able to come to the knowledge of the truth (2 Timothy 3:7)

Our life experiences do not guarantee we will reach any specific level of maturity. Contrary to common belief, neither time nor age insures any measure of maturity. Our maturing growth depends a lot on the quality of our interaction with God, family, friends, and community. We all need encouragement and our maturing growth requires it.

We are generally cautioned against conversations about religion or politics. Participants of the culture of Christ tend to avoid talking about religion per se. Rather than comparing my church with your church, or my set of beliefs with yours, we want to talk about God and the things of God.

We want to ask someone what God is doing in their heart and life. We can share what we are going through in this particular season. We can share what we are hearing and seeing God do in lives. There are times when we need encouragement and times when we are able to give it.

Although mass communication has some value, it is not the most fruitful interaction for most of us. Our most effective interaction is one-on-one and with a few. We can effectively interact and share with our family, friends, and neighbors. We are all called to this type of interaction.

We are created to live and grow within families and communities. Our maturity depends a lot on our interaction with our heavenly Father and with one another.

The ways of God in the culture of Christ help us develop the desire and skill to interact in more healthy ways. We experience a fuller life as we learn to live out the greatest commandment: To fully love God and love one another as family.

As we become more mature children of God, we reflect and resemble the heart character, attitude, and personality of our heavenly Father in more appropriate ways.

Memorize Ephesians 4:15-16:

> *...but speaking the truth in love, we are to grow up in all aspects into Him who is the head, even Christ, from whom the whole body, being fitted and held together by what every joint supplies, according to the proper working of each individual part, causes the growth of the body for the building up of itself in love.*

Questions to Consider:

1. What are some of the "Nod Effects" we experience when we reject God?

2. What did Jesus identify as the central theme and purpose of Scripture?

3. What are some of the godly traits that indicate we are maturing?

Chapter 8

The Way of Forgiving Commissions Us

Irving Berlin once recounted an insightful event in his life:

"One day I hopped into a taxi and we took off for the airport. We were driving in the right lane when suddenly a black car pulled out of a parking space right in front of us. My taxi driver slammed on his brakes, skidded, and missed the other car by inches! The driver of the other car whipped his head around and started yelling at us. My driver just smiled and waved at the guy. My driver was really friendly.

"So I asked, 'Why did you do that? This guy almost ruined your car and sent us to the hospital!'

"This is when my taxi driver taught me what I now call, 'The Law of the Garbage Truck.' He explained that many people are like garbage trucks. They run around full of garbage, full of frustration, full of anger, and full of disappointment. As their garbage piles up, they need a place to dump it and sometimes they'll dump it on you!"

We do not want to take it personally when people dump on

us. We want to just smile, wave, wish them well, and move on. We don't want to accept their garbage and spread it to other people at work, at home, or on the streets.

People walking in the ways of God in the culture of Christ don't let garbage trucks ruin their day. We are learning to love and routinely forgive even the people that tend to dump on us. We pray much for them. But we prefer to have garbage-free days!

As we are lifted into the fellowship of God's presence in the culture of Christ and respond to the influence of the Prince of Peace, we are better equipped to interact with Him and with each other. Our interaction helps us grow and mature so we can more fully reflect and resemble His heart. As we learn to forgive others like God forgives, we, like God, invite people to repent and enter this way of life.

Maintenance Factor

God lovingly births us into life to reflect and resemble His heart's character, attitude and personality (CAP). As a great Father, God readily forgives our imperfect growth process. We must, however, be repentant people who seek to change in order to receive the full benefits of His forgiving and enabling grace.

Throughout history, repentant attitudes were displayed by the lowering of posture. The most elementary involved laying prostrate on the ground or floor. A lesser degree involved dropping to the knees. The more sophisticated method was just to bow the head to indicate submission.

A repentant posture is supported by an attitude that is submissive and open to change. A repentant attitude is the opposite of a prideful one. A prideful attitude maintains a stance to indicate one is above submissive repentance and unwilling to adjust or change.

A repentant admission of error is evidence that we are willing to change and learn to do better. A humble demeanor invites restoration with our heavenly Father and can help restore our other relationships as well.

In the Old Testament, Malachi prophesied that Elijah would come and restore hearts—of children and fathers.

> *Behold, I am going to send you Elijah the prophet before the coming of...the LORD. He will restore the hearts of the fathers to their children and the hearts of the children to their fathers* (Malachi 4:5-6).

Jesus tells us that Malachi's prophesy concerning Elijah spoke of John the Baptist, the voice that preceded and announced the coming of Jesus:

> *"But I say to you that Elijah already came, and they did not recognize him..." Then the disciples understood that He had spoken to them about John the Baptist* (Matthew 17:12-13).

The message of John the Baptist actually encouraged people to repent because God's kingdom reign *is* at hand, right here in front of us.

> *Now in those days John the Baptist came, preaching in the wilderness of Judea, saying, "Repent, for the kingdom of heaven is at hand"* (Matthew 3:1-2).

When Jesus addressed the Jewish leaders, He made it clear that John came to point us to righteous living.

John came to you in the way of righteousness and you did not receive him (Matthew 21:32).

Jesus went on to affirm what was meant by the kingdom of God is "at hand" when He said it is in our midst.

Now having been questioned by the Pharisees as to when the kingdom of God was coming, He answered them and said, "The kingdom of God is not coming with signs to be observed; nor will they say, 'Look, here it is!' or, 'There it is!' For behold, the kingdom of God is in your midst" (Luke 17:20-21).

We want to realize that repentance is a foundational condition for experiencing God among us. Malachi's "restoring of hearts," John's "way of righteousness," and Jesus' "the kingdom of God in our midst" are all related to repentance!

The kingdom of God is one of the names in scripture that refer to the culture of Christ. The rule of God in our life is a function that begins in our repentant heart. Our heart response enables us to see and hear (become more aware of) what God is saying and doing.

A repentant heart allows the reality of God's governing reign to influence our life. God's governing insight keeps us turning from error toward His righteous ways.

Jesus spoke of this affect in the story of a king settling his accounts. When one who owed more than he could repay was about to be sold into servitude for the debt, the man fell to the floor and asked for patience. Then the king felt compassion and forgave the debt.

The forgiven one, to his shame, left the king's presence and went to those who owed him and demanded payment. When the king heard the forgiven one was unforgiving, the servant's forgiveness was revoked (see Matthew 18:23-35).

This story illustrates how God's forgiveness is freely given to repentant people, but it is also meant to teach us to become forgivers. Our humble repentance should produce in us more than an ability to repent. We want to *be* forgivers, people who reflect and resemble the forgiving heart of God, not only in what we do but also in who we are.

Repentant people retain repentant attitudes that allow us to continually access God's presence and partake of the Tree of Life. The Tree of Life is a visual for God's fellowship. This Tree provides us with eternal insights and qualities.

> *Jesus said to them, "I am the way, and the truth, and the life..."* (John 14:6).

> *This is eternal life, that they may know You, the only true God, and Jesus Christ whom You have sent* (John 17:3).

> *As the living Father sent Me, and I live because of the Father, so he who eats* [partakes of] *Me, he also will live because of Me* (John 6:57).

Knowing God and knowing Jesus are much more than knowing of God or acknowledging that Jesus existed. This speaks of a relational knowing that experiences God as Father and Jesus as our example of a life that is properly relating to our heavenly Father. When we go beyond just knowing *about* God and know Him *by experience*, we actually partake of the Tree of Life and eternity.

We maintain our forgiveness by becoming forgivers who forgive as God forgives. His forgiveness of us should affect our overall demeanor, posture, and appearance. As forgiven people, we cease to appear as hateful, demanding, overbearing, prideful, or arrogant. We become better reflections and resemblances of our heavenly Father as we become forgiving people.

Freely you received, freely give (Matthew 10:8).

How Do We Forgive?

Bud had been taken advantage of on the job. His boss saw Bud's desire to please as weakness, so when he needed to have some personal errands run, he always called on Bud. Soon it was getting out of hand, and Bud was falling behind in his work.

When the time came for Bud's annual review, he was denied a raise due to low productivity. Bud went to his boss and told him that he was passed over for a raise because constant errands interrupted his productivity.

Bud's boss apologized and stopped asking Bud to run errands, but the damage was done. No raise. Every time Bud thought about the injustice he felt anger and bitterness. Eventually Bud decided to forgive his boss.

Each morning Bud chose to renew his forgiveness, and before long he noticed he felt less irritation. After a few more weeks he realized he no longer felt bitter, angry, or bothered by his boss. The forgiveness was complete.

When we forgive, we forgive the person, not the offense.

Forgiveness is not an effort to excuse the offense or to receive some sort of restitution. We just trust our heavenly Father to work something good out of it.

When offenses, insults and abuses come, they can create wounds that short circuit our well-being. Hurts can fester and cause us to be angry and bitter. Dwelling on offenses negatively affects on our mental, emotional, and physical health. Carrying grievances create emotional stress and anxieties, which can turn into physical disease. In fact, medical science has found that festering irritations cause many of the cancers that eat away at our health.

> *Why has my pain been perpetual and my wound incurable, refusing to be healed?* (Jeremiah 15:18a)

> *For the heart of this people has become dull, and with their ears they scarcely hear, and they have closed their eyes; otherwise, they might see with their eyes, and hear with their ears, and understand with their heart and return, and I would heal them* (Acts 28:27).

The incurable wounds and perpetual pains we live with are destructive pits that we keep re-digging by not forgiving. When we do not forgive, we insanely choose to be hurt over and over by ill side effects of an offense.

When we forgive those who brought us abuse, we invite the Great Healer to come and root out of us the irritations that eat away at our emotional and physical health. Forgiving is not an option for those who walk in the ways of God in the culture of Christ; it is a necessity.

Then Peter came and said to Him, "Lord, how often shall my brother sin against me and I forgive him? Up to seven times?" Jesus said to him, "I do not say to you, up to seven times, but up to seventy times seven" (Matthew 18:21-22).

The significance of numbers in the Bible provides us with an interesting view of what Jesus told Peter. The number seven represents spiritual perfection, and the number ten signifies divine order. A multiplication of two numbers signifies intensity. Seven times ten equals seventy. This signifies intensified spiritual perfection and divine order.

When Jesus multiplied seven times seventy, He indicated full forgiveness. We want to forgive completely. This can mean a continual forgiving until we are no longer bothered by the offense.

When old offenses have festered for a long time, repetitive efforts to forgive are usually necessary before the irritations we carry are fully uprooted. Each time an offense is remembered, we should forgive until we are totally free of any anger or bitterness. We know forgiveness is complete when we can remember the incident without feeling bitter or angry.

We must consciously choose to forgive again and again until forgiveness has freed us of all ill side effects. We know we have fully forgiven when we can sincerely pray that God will bless the offender.

As we become seasoned forgivers, fresh offenses and potential irritations are even diverted from causing damage, much like water is repelled off the well-known duck's back. Scripture provides many examples: David was cursed, slandered, and stoned; yet, he forgave. The wise Solomon forgave the brother who tried to displace him as king. Stephen was illegally condemned and as they stoned him, he forgave. Jesus forgave His crucifiers as they unjustly ridiculed and tortured him.

> *But Jesus was saying, "Father, forgive them; for they do not know what they are doing"* (Luke 23:34).

As forgiveness is God's invitation for us to repent and change our ways, so our forgiveness of others becomes an invitation for them to repent and change. Everyone makes mistakes. Some are so caught up in their erroneous experience that their mistakes are habitual. We do not want to be held captive in their mess by not forgiving them.

Rise and Shine

Consider the life of Joseph, Jacob's favorite son. He was born into a large family where he shared his father's affections with three other half-families. He was given special status, which made him very unpopular with his half-brothers. After years of verbal abuse by his brothers, he was thrown into a dry well, told he would be killed, and was then sold into slavery. The abandonment by his family was followed by more abuse at the hand of his captors.

If Joseph had not forgiven when mistreatment came, he would have been plagued by anger and bitterness. The ill side effects of not forgiving would have affected his attitude on the job and with each of his relationships. Instead, Joseph's heart and actions appear to be blessed by God. Joseph did not fall victim to family shortcomings, people's mistreatment, or the ill after-effects of not forgiving. Joseph was a forgiver.

> *Joseph said to them, "Do not be afraid, for am I in God's place? As for you, you meant evil against me, but God meant it for good in order to bring about this present result, to preserve many people alive..." So he comforted them and spoke kindly to them* (Genesis 50:19-21).

If we do not forgive, we allow hurts to hold us captive and cause us to respond to one another negatively. Disciplined forgivers do not respond to an offender by judging and condemning. We simply forgive.

To be a forgiver, we must change our fundamental way of thinking and dismiss our natural tendency to condemn. Everyone makes mistakes; it is a part of life, a part of our growing and developing process.

It is also important to realize that our personal attitude toward people is different from that of governing authorities. The government is authorized, even by God, to guard and protect the safety of the group. We, however, are charged with guarding our own personal heart.

See Appendix VIII: No Fear In Love

We receive forgiveness by repenting. We maintain and walk in forgiveness by becoming forgivers. No one can reflect and resemble God very well without following His forgiving lead. Forgivers, as the taxi driver, tend to remain garbage free. God instructs us to learn to forgive one another just like He does, freely and without reserve.

Should you not also have had mercy on your fellow slave, in the same way that I had mercy on you? (Matthew 18:33)

God's forgiveness is not dependent on any of us deserving it. He forgives as a loving invitation for us to repent. As with God, our heartfelt forgiveness is not dependent on anyone deserving it. We forgive for our own sake, for our health, and then as an invitation for others to repent.

Truly I say to you, whatever you bind on earth shall have been bound in heaven and whatever you loose on earth shall have been loosed in heaven (Matthew 18:18).

If you forgive the sins of any, their sins have been forgiven them; if you retain the sins of any, they have been retained (John 20:23).

Our failure to forgive can bind an offender to their problem (at least in our mind). When we treat someone as though they are what they were, we are condemners not forgivers. Our attitude toward them can complicate, restrict, or even reverse their efforts to change. On the other hand, our forgiving character can be as a light to others.

Arise, shine; for your light has come, and the glory of the LORD has risen upon you. For behold, darkness will cover the earth and deep darkness the peoples; but the LORD will arise upon you and His glory will appear upon you. Nations will come to your light, and kings to the brightness of your rising (Isaiah 60:1-3).

People who live by the ways of God in the culture of Christ arise in the light of God. When we become forgivers, as God is, we become shining lights to those dwelling in darkness.

Enabled Ministry

Jesus commissioned us to follow His example and forgive as the Father forgives. When we forgive, we invite restoring repentance.

Jesus even asked us to bear one another's burdens. When we carry one another's burdens, as He did on the cross, we demonstrate to others God's forgiveness and thus fulfill the law of Christ.

Bear one another's burdens, and thereby fulfill the law of Christ (Galatians 6:2).

Jesus amplified this concept when He said our commission is to live as He did, to be peaceful and forgiving expressions of our forgiving heavenly Father.

Jesus said to them again, "Peace be with you; as the Father has sent Me, I also send you" (John 20:21).

God commissions us to be as saviors on Mt. Zion, to be merciful forgivers. We are to light the way for people dwelling outside of the culture of Christ.

And saviors shall come up on mount Zion...and the kingdom shall be the LORD's (Obadiah 1:21 KJV).

Life in the culture of Christ can be very invigorating. As we partake of our heavenly Father's fellowship and mature as children, we become ambassadors of Christ:

Therefore, we are ambassadors for Christ, as though God were entreating through us, we beg you on behalf of Christ, be reconciled to God (2 Corinthians 5:20).

Now all these things are from God, who reconciled us to Himself through Christ and gave us the ministry of reconciliation, namely, that God was in Christ reconciling the world to Himself, not counting their trespasses against them, and He has committed to us the word of reconciliation (2 Corinthians 5:18-19).

Quite often we think ministry is only for the professionals. The word which is translated "ministry" in the New Testament, *diakonia*, is better translated as "service." Everyone reconciled to God is given this ministerial service of reconciling others to God and to each other. Paul couldn't make it clearer than in the following verses:

But to each one of us grace was given according to the measure of Christ's gift (Ephesians 4:7).

As each one has received a special gift, employ it in serving one another as good stewards of the manifold grace of God (1 Peter 4:10).

Diakonia, which is correctly translated as "service" in this verse, can also be rendered as "support." So each of us has the supportive ministry (service) of reconciliation. This simply means we are all equipped by Christ to forgive and love people into the culture of Christ, into the influencing reign of God.

Many years ago a little known preacher went from town to town with his revival tent. He felt called to preach to everyone who would come. At one location, he set up the tent, but when it was time to start the service, no one had arrived.

He asked the Lord, "What do I do?"

He felt God respond, "Conduct the meeting."

After a while one man came and sat down. At the close of the service the young man gave his heart to the Lord. His name: Billy Graham.

Another example is found in the book, *One Touch*. The author, Chris Schimel, tells of an enlightening experience. With his permission, we have condensed it:

"As a Pastor, I continually looked for bigger and better ways to minister. I wanted my life to have significance. One day there was a knock at my office door. When I opened it, a man unfamiliar to me, dressed in a sport coat and tie, asked if he could talk with me. I said okay.

"He spent the next two hours screaming, crying, ranting, and raving about the streets, the city, the world, and all their ills. Then he left. I thought I'd never see him again and hoped I wouldn't. But he kept coming back every few months over the next two and a half years.

"Each time it was a little more bizarre than the time before. I recall resenting the man because he always seemed to come when I was devoting time to growing my ministry. But God didn't allow me to turn him away.

"On the day of his last visit, I was stewing over a major loss of members after a natural disaster. But before he told me he was leaving the area, I carelessly expressed my frustration about my inability to touch people and keep them connected to me.

"His response was, 'I don't know about everyone else, but you have touched me and I will never be the same.' His statement grabbed my heart. It caused me to rethink all my values about reaching the masses. I began to refocus my heart on what is the heart of God: It is the one."

God commissions us to be as saviors on Mt. Zion, to be merciful forgivers. We are to light the way for people dwelling outside of the culture of Christ.

Too often we focus on the big picture. This can be good in order to understand how the Ways of God work together and to find a good balance. Nevertheless, our faithfulness is actually found in the little things we do for each individual "one."

Jesus said it this way:

> *He who is faithful in a very little thing is faithful also in much* (Luke 16:10-11).

> *His master said to him, "Well done, good and faithful... You were faithful with a few things, I will put you in charge of many things; enter into the joy of your master"* (Matthew 25:23).

We are called to focus on being faithful in the little things that we tend to overlook as insignificant: a cup of water for the thirsty, a meal for the hungry, a listening ear for the frustrated, an encouragement to the discouraged, and a freeing gift of forgiveness to the undeserved.

Our ministry of reconciliation, as co-laborers with God in the culture of Christ, starts with forgiving those who offend. As God's ambassadors, we are commissioned to forgive and be non-condemning invitations to repent. When possible, we proclaim God's invitational forgiveness to the masses.

God is at work in us, molding us into His heart character, attitude, and personality, so we can appropriately reflect and resemble Him, as children.

God wants us to be forgivers that forgive without reserve. When we forgive, we allow God's healing grace to bind up our wounds and release us from all ill side effects. Just as God's forgiveness invites us into restoration, so our forgiveness of one another invites repentance and reconciliation. This is our God-given ministry.

We want to stay involved, no matter what age of life we are in. The youth of our early years adds vitality and inspiring creativity to everyone. The midlife years lend encouragement to the youthful and levels of satisfaction to the elderly. Our latter years lend much wisdom to those who build on what we have built on.

God will grace each of us with what we need in our specific season. It may be the grace to go or stay, to sit or stand, to speak or be silent, to lay it down or to pick it up. The important thing is to be ready, willing, and available to follow His lead.

Participants in the culture of Christ seek to fellowship with God and learn to live by the Ways of God. Here is one way we might articulate our primary purpose in life:

My life purpose is to love God and learn to be an expression of His heart. I want to reflect as a mirror and resemble as a son God's character, attitude and personality to everyone within my reach.

Memorize 2 Corinthians 5:18-20:

Now all these things are from God, who reconciled us to Himself through Christ and gave us the ministry of reconciliation, namely, that God was in Christ reconciling the world to Himself, not counting their trespasses against them, and He has committed to us the word of reconciliation. Therefore, we are ambassadors for Christ, as though God were making an appeal through us...be reconciled to God.

Questions to Consider:

1. What holds us captive when we do not forgive?

2. What if an offense was not intended, or our offender repents before God and we don't forgive?

3. Why should forgiveness be given even when it is not requested?

Epilogue

We can all identify with different cultures, each one with their own unique customs, languages, and peculiarities. Personal preferences usually include touches of our parent's ethnic backgrounds. We are all prone to pick and choose which elements of a culture we want to embrace or ignore.

The culture of Christ has been on the earth ever since Jesus introduced it 2000 years ago. This culture is not located in any geographical place, but it can be found most anywhere in the world.

We are all invited to partake of the insightful presence of our heavenly Father in the culture of Christ. We choose, however, just how much we embrace or ignore. When we respond to the guiding light of God's presence among us and become an active part of this culture, we learn to become better expressions of our heavenly Father.

The life Jesus lived confirms the fact that we really can interact with family and each other appropriately while we follow our heavenly Father's guiding insight (see Luke 2:49-51).

After His resurrection from the dead, Jesus said His presence would be among everyone who identifies with Him while interacting with one another.

> *For where two or three have gathered together in My name, I am there in their midst* (Matthew 18:20).

The culture of Christ can be compared to the water vapor that permeates the air we breathe. The natural eye cannot see the vapor until it becomes so dense that it appears as a mist in the air or congeals into water drops. The moisture in the water vapor is a vital ingredient for life. No one can live without it.

The presence of God in the culture of Christ is like the water vapor in the atmosphere. It supports our ability to live as godly people. When two, three, or more people interact in this culture, the presence of God becomes more visible in the natural realm.

This culture of Christ can also be compared to the penetrating activity of a sauna. As we breathe in the water vapor from the air, it works its way through our entire body and then oozes out as a cleansing sweat. In much the same way, we absorb something of God's presence and it affects us (body, soul, and spirit). Then the godly effect is able to ooze out of us as part of our expression.

The ways of God among us are the methods that God uses to influence and transform our lives into people who maturely reflect and resemble His heart. As we partake of the fellowship of His presence and submit to His ways among us, we absorb eternal benefits and progressively change.

While the world around us may not be aware or actively partaking of this culture, they can still be blessed by the spillover fringe benefits of Christ among us.

Our heavenly Father loves every one of us. God wants to be the primary guiding influence in our lives. The ways of God among us help us understand the desire of God's heart to be a presence that dwells with us, among us, and in our midst. Our heavenly Father wants to assist our growth so we can better reflect His heart character, attitude, and personality. This is God's desired intention for each of our lives.

> *He, your Teacher will no longer hide Himself, but your eyes will behold your Teacher. Your ears will hear a word behind you, "This is the way, walk in it"* (Isaiah 30:20-21).

Let us lay aside reaction, judgment, and isolation, and reach out to our neighbors in love and forgiveness, with a view toward reconciliation.

Appendix I: GOD HAS WAYS

Here's a list of the Scriptures that speak of the Ways of God:

God Teaches Us His Ways

Make me know Your ways, O Lord; Teach me Your paths. Lead me in Your truth and teach me (Psalms 25:4-5).

He leads the humble in justice, and He teaches the humble His way (Psalms 25:9).

Teach me Your way, O Lord, and lead me in a level path (Psalms 27:11).

Teach me Your way, O Lord; I will walk in Your truth (Psalms 86:11).

He made known His ways to Moses, His acts to the sons of Israel (Psalms 103:7).

Turn away my eyes from looking at vanity, and revive me in Your ways (Psalms 119:37).

Let us go up…that He may teach us concerning His ways and that we may walk in His paths (Isaiah 2:3).

Let us go up…that He may teach us about His ways and that we may walk in His paths (Micah 4:2).

Teacher, we know that You are truthful and teach the way of God in truth (Matthew 22:16).

Teacher, we know that You are truthful…teach the way of God in truth (Mark 12:14).

Teacher, we know that You speak and teach…the way of God in truth (Luke 20:21).

We Can "Know" the Ways of God

If I have found favor in Your sight, let me know Your ways that I may know You (Exodus 33:13).

That Your way may be known on the earth, Your salvation among all nations (Psalms 67:2).

Make me know Your ways, O Lord; Teach me Your paths (Psalms 25:4).

They are a people who err in their heart, and they do not know My ways (Psalms 95:10).

Then I said... They do not know the way of the Lord (Jeremiah 5:4).

I will go to the great and will speak to them, for they know the way of the Lord (Jeremiah 5:5).

Yet they seek Me day by day and delight to know My ways (Isaiah 58:2).

They always go astray in their heart, and they did not know My ways (Hebrews 3:10).

We Can "Keep" the Ways of God

That he may command his children and his household after him to keep the way of the Lord (Genesis 18:19).

To test Israel... whether they will keep the way of the Lord to walk in it (Judges 2:22).

For I have kept the ways of the Lord, and have not acted wickedly (2 Samuel 22:22).

I have kept the ways of the Lord...have not wickedly departed from my God (Psalms 18:21).

Wait for the Lord and keep His way, and He will exalt you to inherit the land (Psalms 37:34).

We Can "Walk" in the Ways of God

You shall keep the commandments of the LORD your God, to walk in His ways (Deuteronomy 8:6).

What does the LORD your God require from you...to walk in all His ways and love Him, and to serve the LORD your God with all your heart and with all your soul (Deuteronomy 10:12).

For if you are careful...to love the LORD your God, to walk in all His ways (Deuteronomy 11:22).

If you carefully observe...to love the LORD your God, and to walk in His ways always (Deuteronomy 19:9).

You have today declared...and that you would walk in His ways and keep His statutes (Deuteronomy 26:17).

The Lord will establish you...if you...walk in His ways (Deuteronomy 28:9).

See, I have set before you today life and prosperity...to walk in His ways (Deuteronomy 30:15).

The Rock! His work is perfect, for all His ways are just; a God of faithfulness (Deuteronomy 32:4).

Only be very careful...to love the LORD your God and walk in all His ways (Joshua 22:5).

Keep the charge of the LORD your God, to walk in His ways...that you may succeed (1 Kings 2:3).

If you walk in My ways...as your father David walked, then I will prolong your days (1 Kings 3:14).

If you listen to all that I command you and walk in My ways, and do what is right in My sight (1 Kings 11:38).

That He may incline our hearts to Himself, to walk in all His ways (1 Kings 8:58).

That they may fear [revere, reverence] *You, to walk in Your ways as long as they live* (2 Chronicles 6:31).

Oh that My people would listen to Me, that Israel would walk in My ways! (Psalms 81:13)

They also do no unrighteousness; they walk in His ways (Psalms 119:3).

How blessed is everyone who fears the Lord, who walks in His ways (Psalms 128:1).

The Lord, against whom we have sinned, and in whose ways they were not willing to walk? (Isaiah 42:24)

Thus says the Lord of hosts, "If you will walk in My ways" (Zechariah 3:7).

I will be your God, and you will be My people; and you will walk in all the way... (Jeremiah 7:23).

We Can "Teach" the Ways Of God

Create in me a clean heart, O God, and renew a steadfast spirit within me...restore to me the joy of Your salvation and sustain me with a willing spirit. Then I will teach transgressors Your ways, and sinners will be converted to You (Psalms 51:10-13).

Appendix II: BORN AGAIN

"Born again" is a term commonly used today to speak of an initial salvation experience. It was not always so.

Before the early 1700s, the term was rarely if ever used. It was not a doctrine that was taught by Catholics or Protestants. Most ministers were not even familiar with the term. So, what happened that brought the term into common use?

Following the Reformation of the 1500s, Protestant churches taught that no one could be assured of salvation. The doctrine was clear: If we give ourselves to church teaching, do our best, and lead a moral life, we should make it into heaven.

This perception of salvation was better than church teachings before the Reformation, when nearly everyone was condemned to purgatory as a place between heaven and hell. The believer's experience was generally void of emotional encouragement and resembled a works-oriented type of faith.

Cleansing Presence

In the early 1700s, a few ministers became concerned about the lack of feeling and coldness in the church experience. As they sought God for answers, they were reminded of the reformation message of Martin Luther, "Salvation is by faith in Christ, by grace alone." God began to move on them, one by one, with a cleansing presence. The experience left an assurance of God's saving favor. A light came on.

In 1735, the well-known New England theologian Jonathan Edwards was one of the first to experience this cleansing sensation. He introduced his region of America to this soul-stirring experience which usually followed a sincere repentance. Revival broke out in the churches in his area of the country.

In 1736, England's Wesley brothers and George Whitefield were stirred by the same concern. They also experienced a cleansing presence and assurance of God's favor. The Wesleys then stirred revival all over England while Whitefield traveled to America.

Whitefield's messages graphically described the "hell we deserve" and told of the "grace God desires to give." He entreated everyone to "weep before God in repentance and feel His love wash you, as I have, and be born again." People responded and experienced the cleansing sensation.

The meetings began to change people's perception of God and produce a new found faith. Rather than "the distant God" they had been taught about, people began to believe in "a near God." They experienced an emotionally stirring presence which left a cleansed feeling and an assurance of salvation.

Whitefield became a preaching wonder throughout America. He spoke with an uncommon animation and delivered his message with a voice charged full of emotion. During 10 trips, He held 350 meetings in 75 towns and cities, and spoke to over a quarter of America's population (about 800,000).

At one meeting in Boston it was estimated 23,000 people gathered to hear him speak. It was reported that his voice could be heard a quarter of a mile away. What an amazing feat considering microphones and electronic media did not exist!

Established ministers feared Whitefield's preaching was bringing disorder and labeled it emotional babble. The revivals of that day came to be called "The Great Awakening."

Whitefield's message introduced a new thought as he declared: You can be "born again." He said this cleansing presence is as a new birth; it will change your life. This concept comes from just one text in Scripture, in the Gospel of John:

> *Jesus answered: "Truly, truly, I say to you, unless one is born again, he cannot see the kingdom of God." Nicodemus said to Him, "How can a man be born when he is old? He cannot enter a second time into his mother's womb and be born, can he?" Jesus answered, "...I say to you, unless one is born of water and the Spirit, he cannot enter into the kingdom of God. That which is born of the flesh is flesh, and that which is born of the Spirit is spirit. Do not be amazed that I said to you, 'You must be born again.' The wind blows where it wishes and you hear the sound of it, but do not know where it comes from and where it is going; so is everyone who is born of the Spirit"* (John 3:1-8).

The cleansing experience of the day came to be known as a rebirth, a born again conversion. People even began to ask one another if they had been born again. New churches sprang up that proclaimed this experience was required for salvation.

Upon close examination, we discover the phrase has a much grander meaning. The Greek word, *anothen*, in these verses is translated as "again." Anothen is a combination of *ano*, which means "above" and the suffix *then*, which means "from." The word actually means "from above."

The King James Version translated anothen in each instance as "from above," except in this text we are examining. (The other verses are: John 3:31; James 1:17; John 19:11; Matthew 27:50-51; Mark 15:38; Luke 1:3; Acts 26:5; John 19:23; Hebrews 10:5, 8.)

Clearly Nicodemus did not have a clue about what Jesus was saying. So we should not assume his idea of being born again has any kind of bearing on what Jesus was saying. In this text, Jesus said the kingdom of God is not seen or entered into (perceived or experienced) without receiving Spirit input from above.

Ascribing to a belief system as Nicodemus did (Judaism), does not mean that any one is experiencing God's governing presence. Jesus encouraged us to receive from God's Spirit so we can perceive and experience God's kingdom reign in our lives.

The kingdom of God is a fellowship of hearts, His with ours and ours with others. Our repentant approach toward God submits our heart to His governing presence. This is true for any one in any generation. Our heavenly Father desires to lead and guide us through life. The emotionally stirring and cleansing experience began to spark this reality in people's lives.

The "born from above" concept is really introduced earlier in John's first chapter.

> *As many as received Him...He gave the right to become*
> *children* [teknon] *of God, even to those who believe in*
> *His name, who were born, not of blood nor of the will of*

the flesh, nor of the will of man, but of God (John 1:12-13).

Each person is an offspring of God. We all have with us the potential to be children that are disciplined by our heavenly Father. This potential, however, is like an image contained in a piece of wood waiting for the artist to cut it out. Our repentant acceptance of God in Christ gives us the right to be taught and trained by the Father as governed children.

Teknon Vs. Huios

The Greek word *teknon* (children) in the Jewish culture spoke of the formative years of a child. Hebrew men were considered to be forming children until the age of thirty. Boys passed through two stages of childhood before they were considered mature adults. The first stage involved twelve years under a mother's care until the Bar-mitzvah. This first process was not without a father's involvement, but the mother was the primary, everyday teacher. The second stage was under the father's care and the instruction of tutors until the age of thirty, when he was then considered an adult, a mature son.

Scripture translates another Greek word *huios* as "child" and "son." This word is not like teknon; it indicates an adult level of maturity. Huios was only used of men who had reached the age of thirty. Jesus entered public ministry at the age of thirty. Jesus spoke of Himself as the "huios (mature child) of man," while others called him the "huios (mature son) of God." He was called teknon only once, by His mother.

The distinction between the Greek words teknon and huios is

very obvious in Romans 8:14-21. Paul speaks of elementary believers as teknon (forming children), while he identifies those who are following the Spirit of God as huios (mature child).

> For all who are being led by the Spirit of God, these are [huios - mature] sons of God...The Spirit Himself testifies with our spirit that we are [tekon - forming] children of God, and if [tekon - forming] children, heirs also, heirs of God and fellow heirs with Christ...

> For the anxious longing of the creation waits eagerly for the revealing of the [huios - mature] sons of God...in hope that the creation itself also will be set free from its slavery to corruption into the freedom of the glory of the [tekon - forming] children of God (Romans 8:14-21).

Humans are offspring of God that are under the disciplines of the natural realm. Many call the planet we live on "Mother Earth." God is involved in the life of all His offspring, but not quite like He is when we accept Him as our governing Father.

Those who see and respond to any of the disciplines of the Father's guidance are forming children (teknon) who are in a process of becoming mature children (huios). Our "birth from above" includes an ongoing process of learning to be Spirit-led people. Scripture does not indicate our development is restricted to any specific time frame.

From a biblical perspective, our "birth from above" is much more than an event; it's an ongoing forming process, a "receiving from above." When we receive from our heavenly Father, we actually see and enter into the experience of the kingdom of God and partake of the governance of the Father. When we view "born from above" as a "born again" event, we can overlook God's governing and formative intent.

With the above insights in mind, the two texts in the Gospel of John that introduce the "born from above" concept could read as such:

> *All who believe and receive Christ, to them God gives permission to be formed and developed as growing children... who are governed by Father* (John 1:12-13, Christ Culture paraphrase).

> *Jesus answered... "Truly, truly, I say to you, unless you actively receive from above, you cannot comprehend the governing reign of God in your life...unless you are responsive in flesh and spirit, you are not experiencing God's governing guidance. He that responds to the flesh is natural and he that responds to the Spirit is spiritual. Don't be amazed that I said, 'You must actively respond to God.' The wind blows where it wants and you hear the sound of it, but do not know where it comes from and where it is going; so it is with everyone who actively responds to the Spirit of God"* (John 3:3, 6-8, Christ Culture paraphrase).

Jesus said those who respond to the Spirit of God are responsive in spirit and flesh. Our response is not just in spirit, it includes our flesh as well. Jesus even said we cannot always know who is or is not responding for they are as indiscernible as blowing wind. We only know by the effects, by the fruit of their life (see Matthew 7:16).

151

Forming children (teknon) of God are offspring of God who receive and respond to the governing, forming, and maturing guidance of our Father. Children partake of the kingdom reign of God as they receive His guiding insight.

It is obvious that maturity does not mean that we are mature in each area of life, at all times, or in every situation. The most mature (huios) sons still experience further maturing processes. Even the Apostle Paul admitted:

> *I do not regard myself as having laid hold of it yet...one thing I do: forgetting what lies behind and reaching forward to what lies ahead, I press on toward the goal for the prize of the upward call of God in Christ* (Philippians 3:13-14).

George Washington understood his spiritual life was a developmental process. He wrote in his journal: "Oh, eternal and everlasting God, direct my thoughts, words, and work. Wash away my sins...and purge my heart by the Holy Spirit. Daily, frame me more and more in the likeness of thy Son, Jesus Christ."

I gave my heart to God as a pre-teen. During my teenage years, I read the Scriptures daily and asked many questions which resulted in several short conversations with God. One evening while on a walk, I recalled some of the amazing conversions I'd heard. These were life-changing events that people had as they began to respond to God.

As I thought about these amazing experiences, I asked God if I was missing part of His purpose for my life. Should I know life without Him, as a Prodigal, so I could also experience a conversion event? Would this give me a greater appreciation of His love?

I sensed God say, "You have chosen the better way." I immediately understood it is much better to learn to walk with God from our beginnings than it is to live in separation and eventually come to a sudden awakening that turns us to God's governing guidance.

We might begin to perceive and experience the kingdom of God in a major awakening event. Or we can realize through a series of waking moments that God is speaking, sharing insight, leading, and guiding. It does not matter how we begin to respond to our heavenly Father, the important thing is that we be receptive to the Spirit of God throughout life.

A "birth from above" really speaks of our ongoing response to the governance of God. Are we allowing Him to teach, discipline and bring us into mature reflections and resemblances of His heart? Are we resting in a born-from-above experience (good), or are we responding daily to the governing reign of God in our life (better)?

Appendix III: GOD'S JUDGMENTS

Years ago, some errand boys were whistling as they went about their work through the streets of London. An alert musician noticed the boys were whistling off-key. After investigating, he discovered the bells of Westminster Abbey were ringing slightly out of tune as well. The boys were just copying what they heard every day.

This is a picture of what is happening in this generation. Many of us are living off-key because of the erroneous perceptions we've picked up from the world and in some houses of worship.

God is most often depicted as a King or a Judge who is more than ready to cast us aside into a tormenting and unending punishment. We have learned to live with a perception of God that is something like the infamous literary character Dr. Jekyll and Mr. Hyde.

As with the fictional character, God most often appears to have a split personality that can be very gracious at times and rather cruel at other times. We are generally taught that God is ready to cast us into everlasting punishment if we fail to respond to His love. We are often torn between a God that can both love and disdain us. What a distorted picture of our heavenly Father!

No wonder we treat each other as we do! We are under the impression that our love-hate reaction to each other is normal because this is the way God is with us. Our confusion about the nature of God inappropriately seems to give us license to reflect and resemble Him as an angry God who is ready to destroy those who disagree with Him.

Does God have any resemblance to a dark side? Scripture tells us that God is love and He is motivated only by the love that makes up His nature (see 1 John 4:7-8, 16). God does not even produce a shadow (see James 1:17). The only dark side of God is in our confused perception of Him.

If God really is Love, how should we view His judgments? Scripture reveals that God's judgments are really like the fatherly disciplines that are meant to correct wayward children.

> *God deals with you as with sons…we had earthly fathers to discipline us, and we respected them; shall we not much rather be subject to the Father of spirits…He disciplines us for our good* (Hebrews 12:5-13). Read Psalms 19:7-11.

> *My son, do not reject the discipline of the Lord or loathe His reproof, for whom the Lord loves He reproves, even as a father corrects the son in whom he delights* (Proverbs 3:11-12).

> *Behold, how happy is the man whom God reproves, so do not despise the discipline of the Almighty* (Job 5:17).

The judgments of God are corrective actions. Each of His judgments are expressions of love that are meant to remove the sinful dross that infects us and stains us.

God's love freely forgives. We just need to repent and receive it. When we do not accept His forgiving kindness, our heavenly Father may extend His grace and mercy in ways that can appear to be harsh judgment, lest we continue in our erroneous way of life. He really loves us!

Remember, God removed Adam and Eve from the Garden of Eden so they would not eat of the Tree of Life while they were unrepentant. Expulsion was God's merciful action to bring them to repentance. We receive the life-restoring benefits of forgiveness when we are repentant, give up our destructive behavior, and submit to God and His way of life.

God hates sin but not the sinner. God's wrath is only against our iniquity and sinful ways, not against us. Yes, Scripture even tells us that "our God is a consuming fire" (Hebrews 12:29; Deuteronomy 4:24). The fire of God's love is not meant to destroy us but to destroy the impurities in us. God wants to purge the dross from our lives and, as through a smelter's fire, bring us forth as pure silver and gold (see Malachi 3:3).

Yes, at times, we can be hurt by accidents, error, and the ill intentions of others. Our suffering can also be the result of our stubborn ways. These are not necessarily God inspired. When we submit to God, we become recipients of His loving corrections.

So why are we taught to fear the Lord? A well-known verse used to support such is:

> The fear of the Lord is the beginning of wisdom, and the knowledge of the Holy One is understanding (Proverbs 9:10).

The Hebrew word translated fear in this verse means "reverence," which is a deep respect mixed with awe and wonder. A few versions translate the word correctly, as reverence (*The Living Bible, J.B. Phillips New Testament, Good News Translation*, and *Rotherham's Emphasized Bible*).

God does not want us to have a dreadful fear of Him. This

verse is really saying, "The reverence and knowledge of the Lord is the beginning of wisdom and understanding." A reverence of God nurtures our trust and confidence in our heavenly Father's love and good will toward each of us.

There is no dark side of God. Let's toss away our Jekyll and Hyde perception. Can we accept His disciplines as the corrective hand of our loving heavenly Father?

Appendix IV: THE POWER OF HUMILITY

George Washington Carver was the scientist who developed hundreds of useful products from the peanut. Late in life, he reported:

"When I was young, I said to God, 'God, tell me the mystery of the universe.' But God answered, 'That knowledge is reserved for me alone.' So I said, "God, tell me the mystery of the peanut.' Then God answered and said, 'Well, George, that's more nearly your size.' And He told me."

Jesus did say that if we seek, we will find (see Luke 11:9). George was initially asking for insight that was beyond his ability to understand. When he humbly scaled his request down to what he could understand and could be useful, God accommodated him.

Scripture compares humility with pride and identifies pride as the opposite of humility. Pride is a self-lifting attitude while humility tends to shy away from boasting.

> *Pride goes before destruction and a haughty spirit before stumbling. It is better to be humble in spirit with the lowly than to divide the spoil with the proud* (Proverbs 16:18-19).

> *A man's pride will bring him low, but a humble spirit will obtain honor* (Proverbs 29:23).

Pride is not a bad thing in and of itself; a certain amount of pride is a good thing. When we consider how we are offspring of God, we become aware that we are something of value. Many of us are being trained by the Father as children who more closely represent His character, attitude, and personality (CAP). This places great value on our life, but it is not a reason or an excuse to be prideful.

John Flavel, a clergyman of the late 1600s once said: "They that know God will be humble and they that know themselves cannot be proud." Too much pride can complicate humility and, in essence, complicate our lives.

Scripture equates humility with repentance. Pride entertains an unrepentant attitude of superiority while humility causes us to withdraw in modest reserve.

> *Remember all the way which the Lord your God has led you in the wilderness these forty years, that He might humble you, testing you...In the wilderness He fed you manna which your fathers did not know, that He might humble you and that He might test you, to do good for you in the end* (Deuteronomy 8:2-3, 16).

> *If...My people who are called by My name humble themselves and pray and seek My face and turn from their wicked ways, then I will hear from heaven, will forgive their sin and will heal their land* (2 Chronicles 7:13-14).

> *Hezekiah humbled the pride of his heart, both he and the inhabitants of Jerusalem* (2 Chronicles 32:26).

Humility is visible evidence of a repentant person. The humble heart will quickly apologize and in repentance, seek to change and make amends. A humble person also tends to recognize his shortcomings and is open to receive additional insight. God instructs and teaches His ways to the humbly repentant person.

Remember, O Lord, Your compassion and Your loving-kindnesses [forgiveness], *for they have been from of old …Good and upright is the Lord; therefore He instructs sinners in the way. He leads the humble in justice, and He teaches the humble His way* (Psalms 25:6, 8-9).

My soul will make its boast in the Lord; the humble will hear it and rejoice. O, magnify the Lord with me, and let us exalt His name together (Psalms 34:2-3).

Thus says the LORD, "Heaven is My throne and the earth is My footstool. Where then is a house you could build for Me? And where is a place that I may rest? For My hand made all these things…" declares the LORD. "But to this one I will look, to him who is humble and contrite of spirit, and who trembles at My word" (Isaiah 66:1-2).

Humility assumes we are not as good as we could be while pride assumes we are better than we really are. Anything in the humble person that may resemble pride is really a respectful honor of another, generally of our heavenly Father.

When we are humble, we allow God to raise us into a more appropriate honor. When God elevates the humble, any sense of honor is quickly deflected to the one who allowed or caused the elevation.

God is opposed to the proud, but gives grace to the humble. Humble yourselves in the presence of the Lord, and He will exalt you (James 4:6, 10).

Clothe yourselves with humility toward one another, for God is opposed to the proud, but gives grace to the humble.

Therefore humble yourselves under the mighty hand of God, that He may exalt you at the proper time, casting all your anxiety on Him, because He cares for you (1 Peter 5:5-7).

To sum up, all of you be harmonious, sympathetic, brotherly, kindhearted, and humble in spirit (1 Peter 3:8).

Humility is more than a powerful ally. Our humility is a powerful safeguard against many adversities.

Appendix V: AGENT OF CHANGE

God is defined in Scripture as: eternal (always, before and after), omnipresent (in attendance everywhere), omnipotent (almighty, all-powerful), omniscient (all-knowing), and invisible (unseen to natural eye).

God does not change; He is as He is (see Malachi 3:6-7). Despite our perceptions, God does not even vary enough to produce a shifting shadow (see James 1:17).

When God speaks, He expresses desire as a spoken word. God's spoken word is the articulated expression that goes forth from His being, to reveal the intention of His mind and the desire of His heart (see Isaiah 55:10-11).

While God does not change, His spoken word is actually an agent of change. When God speaks, change happens. Scripture says the spoken word of God is not static or motionless—it is living and active (see Hebrews 4:12). God's spoken word is described as spirit and life (see John 6:63), to those that receive them (see Luke 8:10-15 and James 1:21-25).

The spoken words of God are alive, active, and motion-filled expressions that reveal light and love (see John 1:1-4). When God expresses desire, an energetic motion proceeds from His being as a word and change happens.

For as the rain and the snow come down from heaven, and do not return there without watering the earth and making it bear and sprout, and furnishing seed to the sower and bread to the eater; So will My word be which goes forth from My mouth; it will not return to Me empty, without accomplishing what I desire, and without succeeding in the matter for which I sent it (Isaiah 55:10-11).

Heaven and earth will pass away, but My words will not pass away [without accomplishing its intent] (Matthew 24:35).

When God decided to become a parent, He spoke and His word went forth and created a vast material universe of changing activity. Eventually the earth formed and took shape to become the place where God would birth and initially train His offspring to reflect and resemble Him.

You, Lord, in the beginning laid the foundation of the earth, and the heavens are the works of your hands (Hebrews 1:10).

God created the heavens and the earth...Then God said... and God made (Genesis 1:1-3). (Verses 1-26 show the progress.)

The heavens are the work of Thy hands...thou wilt change them...but Thou art the same (Psalm 102:25-27 and Hebrews 1:10-11).

In the beginning of the time and space material realm, the word of God was with God as the spoken expression of God. In this capacity, the word of God is as God because God's expression carries the authority of God Himself.

In the beginning was the Word, and the Word was with God, and the Word was God. He was in the beginning with God. All things came into being through Him, and apart from Him nothing came into being that has come into being (John 1:1-3).

As the Eternal One's agent, the creative word of God goes forth to bring into reality His expressed will. The spoken word makes known God's desire by creating, revealing, making, and forming through processes of change.

The spoken word of God has come to mankind throughout human history in a variety of forms. God's word reveals and manifests His will in time and space by appearing in whatever form is needed for a particular situation.

There have been times when God's spoken word appeared as an angel, as a man, as a written message on a wall, as thunder and lightning, even as a series of events foretold by Daniel, Ezekiel, and John. The spoken word of God has been heard by men as a still small voice and as a thunderous sound (see 1 Kings 19:12-13 and Exodus 20:18-19). Even the angelic hosts are sent as messengers to deliver God's word (see Psalms 104:4 and Hebrews 1:7).

When Sarah was past childbearing age, God spoke and told Abraham that he and Sarah would have a son. While this promised son was growing up, God spoke and instructed Abraham to sacrifice his son as an offering to God. Abraham proceeded to be obedient and do as instructed. When Abraham was ready to slay him, God in essence said, "Do not do what I told you to do" (see Genesis 22).

If Abraham did not believe that God's word of instruction could change, he would have just obeyed yesterday's word and slain his son. The word of God promised a son, instructed the son to be slain, and then spared the son from the death sentence. God's word to us can and does change. We want to be obedient to what we hear today.

Centuries later, Abraham's faith offspring was known as the nation of Israel (see Galatians 3:1-7, 14, 26-29 and Romans 4:1-16). God miraculously delivered them from Egyptian slavery and then led them through a wilderness desert.

For two years Israel supernaturally received daily supplies of water out of a rock, manna from the ground, quail from the sky, and even victory in war. They received the Ten Commandments, a system of worship, and guidelines for corporate life. It was an amazing journey!

When Israel arrived at the borders of the Promise, God instructed them to go in and take it for victory was assured. Israel, however, had not learned to believe that God would help them do as He instructed. Instead, they wanted to return to slavery rather than participate in warfare.

As a result, God's word to them changed. They were told to stay in the desert and die, for His promise would be fulfilled in the next generation. Realizing their error, they dressed for battle, went into the land, and were slaughtered (see Numbers 14 and Deuteronomy 9). Victory was no longer assured for that generation.

As with Abraham and Israel, the spoken word to us may change, depending on our response to His instruction. God's word to Abraham changed because of his obedience, while the word to Israel changed because of disbelief.

We can hear and receive God's word from any of the three forms that are available to us. We can read what God has said in the written word of Scripture (see John 5:39). We can observe the human example in the incarnate word of Jesus Christ (see John 1:14 and 1 John 1:1). We can also sense what the word of God is saying in the still small voice of the Holy Spirit (see 1 Kings 19:12-13 and John 15:26).

> *Since therefore it remains for some to enter it, and those who formerly had good news preached to them failed to enter because of disobedience* [old Israel], *He again fixes a certain day, "Today," saying through David after so long a time, just has been said before, "Today if you hear His voice, do not harden you hearts..." Let us therefore be diligent* [attentive, hardworking, and industrious] *to enter that rest, less anyone fall through, following the same example of disobedience* (Hebrews 4:6-7, 11).

> *Be diligent to present yourself approved to God as a workman...accurately handling* [rightly dividing] *the word of truth* (2 Timothy 2:15).

We want to be attentive to what God is saying today and become obedient to what we understand today, for tomorrow, His word to us may very well change. If we are not following what we hear today, we may not like what we hear tomorrow.

God sends His word to us as an agent of change. God's word to us can bring change into our current situation and His word to us can change depending on our acceptance of what He said to our heart yesterday.

We want to stay sensitive to God's words and attentive to what he is saying and doing today. Our unchanging God is an agent of change.

Appendix VI: SEPARATING INFLUENCE

The scriptural account of creation reveals that God used separations to create variables. The separations were not intended to restrict or devalue anything but rather were made for the purpose of producing a specific value that would contribute its unique gifting to the larger purpose.

When God created the natural universe and formed the earth, He made many distinctions. Among them, He separated light from darkness, the waters above from the waters below, and mankind into male and female (see Genesis 1:4-31).

God separated to create differences, so each could uniquely contribute something to a greater value. Light was separated from darkness to frame day and night. Water was separated from land so the earth would be an inhabitable planet.

The crowning glory of the creation came as God created mankind by separating one being into two—male and female. The distinction equips us to assist God in birthing and growing His offspring. As offspring of God, we all have value that contributes to the function of the family of God.

God not only created separations, He also created instrumental factors to influence separation.

> *Behold, I Myself have created the smith who blows the fire of coals and brings out a weapon for its work; and I have created the destroyer to ruin* (Isaiah 54:16).

The word "destroyer" is translated from a Hebrew verb *shachath*, which means to harm in some manner, as to decay, destroy, and ruin. Shachath is a verb not a noun; it is an action, not a thing or person. The destroyer is not the smith, the coals, or the fire. The destroying factor is the combined activity of the trio. God says He created the destroyer as an instrument to accomplish a specific result.

The purpose of this destroying action is to bring the object into such a state that it can be formed and molded into a more useful product. The activity is only intended to harm the unyielding characteristic in the metal, not the metal itself.

The metal in this metaphor represents our lives, and the destructive activity is intended to assist our development into greater levels of usefulness. God intends the destroying influence to encourage our growth and development.

Scripture also identifies the smelting process as a separating influence. In this example metal ore is placed in extreme heat to extract the ore, gasses, slag, and rock that contaminate the precious metal. The metal can be further refined through additional heating processes.

> For He is like a refiner's fire and like fullers' soap. He will sit as a smelter and purifier of silver, and He will purify the sons...and refine them like gold and silver, so that they may present to the Lord offerings in righteousness (Malachi 3:2-3).

As with the smelting process, God uses life's trials and testing to separate from us non-Christlike characteristics. These trying times increase our growth into refined reflections and resemblances of God's character, attitude, and personality.

In the biblical story of the righteous Job, a presence appeared before God and noted how God restricted harmful activity. When the ability to inflict more harm was increased, it still had restrictions (see Job 1:6-12; 12:16). This presence called Satan was obviously very subordinate to its Creator.

God allowed harmful activity to come to Job so He could extract the small amount of distrust that remained in him (see Job 1:5). This influence acted as a proving agent that sought to separate Job from God. In the end of the story, Job was more refined and better off than before.

The first proving influence to appear in human history came as a crafty serpent in the Garden of Eden. This influence twisted God's word and offered an alternate way of life, indicating that if we ignore God's guidance, we will be as God:

> *The serpent was more crafty than any beast of the field which the LORD GOD had made. And he said to the woman, "Indeed, has God said, 'You shall not eat from any tree of the garden'?"...And the serpent said to the woman, "You surely will not die! For God knows that in the day you eat from it your eyes will be opened, and you will be like God, knowing good and evil"* (Genesis 3:1-5).

The temptation was articulated in the form of three thoughts: 1) "Didn't God say you can eat from any tree?"; 2) "You won't really die"; and 3) suggested they would get what God intended, "God knows that listening to me will make you as God."

When they accepted these ideas, their view of God's relational intent clouded their understanding. Their perception caused them to want to cover up in each other's presence and try to hide from God. When their error was exposed, they shifted blame onto the tempting influence.

The perception continues to skew our understanding and complicates our response to God and one another. We tend to self-protect and hide when we feel guilt. Then when we are exposed, we try to justify our actions. Like Adam and Eve, we are quick to say, "The devil made me do it," or that our spouse or parents are at fault. Such is life when separated from our true source of life.

These Old Testament examples reveal two insights: 1) God created separation to distinguish things for specific relational purposes; and 2) God allows temptation and difficulty as a means of testing and trying us, as proving factors that are really intended to help us mature as His children.

The New Testament Scripture calls this presence that tempts us "the devil" 38 times and "Satan" 34 times. Since the oldest copies of the New Testament are in Greek, it helps to understand the Greek meanings of these words. (Greek is still considered the most descriptive and precise of languages.)

Tempter—(*peirazo*, Strong's Greek #3985); to prove by solicitation; verify one is or is not; to make more so

The devil—(*diabolos*, Strong's Greek #1228); accuser, slanderer, who falsely accuses in order to divide

Satan—(*satanas*, Strong's Greek #4567); to oppose, pit against, an adversary

Temptations come to refine us. They can appear as adversaries that oppose, using slander and accusation. Their purpose, however, is to prove us and reveal to us our level of refinement. We must realize that God already knows our level of maturity. We are the ones in need of clarifying insight.

The same thoughts that Adam and Eve succumbed to confronted the second Adam, Jesus Christ (see 1 Corinthians 12:45). This time the temptation was not visualized as a serpent. Instead, the influence is called tempter, the devil, and Satan.

Jesus was led up by the Spirit into the wilderness to be tempted by the devil. And after He had fasted His forty days and forty nights, He then became hungry. And the tempter came and said to Him, "If You are the Son of God, command these stones to become bread..." and "If You are the Son of God throw yourself down..." [God will protect you] *and "I will give You, if You fall down and worship me." Then Jesus said to him, "Go, Satan! For it is written, 'You shall worship the LORD your God, and serve Him only'"* (Matthew 4:1-11).

As with Adam and Eve, the influence claimed: "If you are God's Son, provide for yourself"; "Test God to prove Him"; and, "If you submit, you'll get what God promised."

Adam accepted these ideas and tried to live separate from their Father. Jesus, however, acknowledged the tempter's purpose was to worship and serve God. This knowledge helped Jesus overcome the temptation to separate, and God remained Lord of His thoughts, feelings, attitude, and actions.

The tempting influence can appear as contrasting thoughts, ideologies, a spirit or angel of light, an attitude, or a critical element in conversation. Many times a person will function as its agent.

God openly encourages some relational separations so He can

bring us into greater levels of maturity. God can lead us to leave a situation we are in or a seasonal stage of life.

> *Then the Lord God said, "It is not good for the man to be alone...For this cause a man shall leave his father and his mother, and cleave to his wife; and they shall become one flesh"* (Genesis 2:18, 24).

Men are instructed to separate from parental beginnings so they can properly partner with a wife in marriage. This is not meant to divide families but to help men fully enter the unique oneness of a spousal relationship.

God can also ask us to leave our extended family and homeland so He can enrich our experience and enlarge our impact, as He did with Abram.

> *The Lord said to Abram, "Go forth from your country, and from your relatives and from your father's house...and I will bless you...And in you all the families of the earth will be blessed"* (Genesis 12:1-3).

During the last days with His disciples, Jesus instructed them to separate from their Jewishness and baptize (immerse) people into His name—into His identifiable presence.

> *And Jesus came up and spoke to them, saying "Go therefore and make disciples of all the nations, baptizing them in the name of the Father and the Son and the Holy Spirit"* (Matthew 28:18-19).

It is also be helpful to realize that our life in God's fellowship is not meant to separate us from the world we live in. Any separation is meant to refine and mature us so we are equipped to more effectively draw others into this way of life.

I do not ask You to take them out of the world, but to keep them from the evil...They are not of the world, even as I am not of the world...As You sent Me into the world, I also have sent them (John 17:15-18).

While our obedient response to God's lead can have a temporary adverse effect on family, friends, and fellowships, it will ultimately enrich our relationship with God and with everyone we touch. When God dwells in our midst as a guiding presence, we can even be distinguished from the religious norm (see Luke 17:11-18).

We want to remember that God is supreme and can bring a good result out of everything. This is especially true for those who love Him (see Romans 8:28). While Adam and Eve's choice was an error, it opened the door for mankind to know God's forgiveness and way of salvation. The Prodigal Son's choice to leave his father equipped him to return and have a better appreciation of his father's care.

God allows both good and bad influences in our lives to act as proofing activities. As servants of God, they are intended to strengthen our resolve toward God and the fellowship of His presence.

Appendix VII: ONE ANOTHER

And one of them, a lawyer, asked Him [Jesus] a question, testing Him, "Teacher, which is the great commandment of the Law?" And He said to him, "'You shall love the Lord your God with all your heart, and with all your soul, and with all your mind.' This is the great and foremost commandment.

"The second is like it, 'you shall love your neighbor as yourself.' On these two commandments depend the whole Law and the Prophets" (Matthew 22:35-40).

This passage is repeated in Luke 10:25-28 and Mark 12:28-3. When Jesus identified the great commandment, He said in essence that it had two parts—we are to love God and each other as well.

To that generation, "all the Law and Prophets" meant all Scripture. Jesus said all Scripture depends on, rests on, and comes down to this two-pronged instruction. God gave the scriptural record of His dealings with man to teach us how to properly love God and love one another.

The gospel of Luke says the lawyer responded to Jesus' comment with, "Who is my neighbor?" as though the lawyer wanted to justify his discriminatory love.

In response, Jesus told him about the Good Samaritan. The Jews of that day hated the Samaritans, considering them to be no better than dogs. Jesus used what was considered the most despised person to illustrate His point. In essence, Jesus said, "Quit qualifying who is your neighbor. Just go and be a good neighbor to those within your reach."

This love thy neighbor feature of the Great Commandment is repeated in Scripture many times, with many variations. Take a few minutes to read them:

If, however, you are fulfilling the royal law according to the Scripture, "You shall love your neighbor as yourself," you are doing well (James 2:8).

Through love, serve one another. For the whole Law is fulfilled in one word, in the statement, "You shall love your neighbor as yourself" (Galatians 5:13b-14).

Owe nothing...except to love one another; for he who loves his neighbor has fulfilled the law (Romans 13:8).

For this, "you shall not commit adultery, you shall not murder, you shall not steal, you shall not covet," and if there is any other commandment, it is summed up in this saying, "you shall love your neighbor as yourself." Love does no wrong to a neighbor; therefore, love is the fulfillment of the law (Romans 13:9-10).

"You have heard that it was said, 'You shall love your neighbor and hate your enemy.' But I say to you, love your enemies and pray for those who persecute you, so that you may be sons of your Father who is in heaven...For if you love those who love you, what reward do you have? Do not even the tax collectors do the same? Therefore you are to be perfect, as your heavenly Father is perfect" (Matthew 5:43-48).

Let no one seek his own good, but that of his neighbor... Give no offense either to Jews or to Greeks or to the church of God; just as I also please all men in all things, not seeking my own profit but the profit of the many, so that they may be saved. Be imitators of me, just as I also am of Christ (1 Corinthians 10:24, 32-11:1).

Now we who are strong ought to bear the weaknesses of those without strength and not just please ourselves. Each of us is to please his neighbor for his good, to his edification (Romans 15:1-3a).

A new commandment I give to you, that you love one another, even as I have loved you, that you also love one another. By this all men will know that you are My disciples, if you have love for one another (John 13:34-35).

This is My commandment, that you love one another, just as I have loved you. Greater love has no one than this; that one lay down his life for his friends (John 15:12-13).

This I command you, that you love one another (John 15:17).

And this is His commandment, that we...love one another, just as He commanded us (1 John 3:23).

Beloved, let us love one another, for love is from God; and everyone who loves is born of God and knows God...for God is love...Beloved, if God so loved us, we also ought to love one another. No one has seen God at any time; if we love one another, God abides in us, and His love is perfected in us (1 John 4:7-8, 11-12).

Now as to the love of the brethren, you have no need for anyone to write to you, for you yourselves are taught by God to love one another; for indeed you do practice it toward all the brethren (1 Thessalonians 4:9-12).

For this is the message which you have heard from the beginning, that we should love one another (1 John 3:11).

Now I ask you, lady, not as though I were writing to you a new commandment, but the one which we have had from the beginning, that we love one another (2 John 1:5).

Fervently love one another from the heart, for you have been born again (1 Peter 1:22).

Above all, keep fervent in your love for one another, because love covers a multitude of sins. Be hospitable to one another without complaint. As each one has received a special gift, employ it in serving one another as good stewards of the manifold grace of God (1 Peter 4:8-10).

Therefore encourage one another and build up one another, just as you also are doing...Live in peace with one another. We urge you, brethren, admonish the unruly, encourage the fainthearted, help the weak, be patient with everyone...always seek after that which is good for one another and for all people (1 Thessalonians 5:11,13b-15).

But encourage one another day after day, so that none of you will be hardened (Hebrews 3:13).

Let us consider how to stimulate one another to love and good deeds, not forsaking our own assembling together, as is the habit of some, but encouraging one another (Hebrews 10:24).

Let us not judge one another anymore, but rather determine this—not to put an obstacle or a stumbling block in a brother's way...So then we pursue the things, which make for peace and the building up of one another (Romans 14:1).

You yourselves are full of goodness, filled with all knowledge and able also to admonish one another (Romans 15:14).

Let the word of Christ richly dwell within you, with all wisdom teaching and admonishing one another with psalms and hymns and spiritual songs, singing with thankfulness in your hearts to God (Colossians 3:14-16).

Speaking to one another in psalms and hymns and spiritual songs, singing and making melody with your heart to the Lord; always giving thanks for all things...and be subject to one another in the fear of Christ (Ephesians 5:19-21).

Be devoted to one another in brotherly love; give preference to one another in honor (Romans 12:10).

Bear one another's burdens, and thereby fulfill the law of Christ (Galatians 6:1-2).

Put on a heart of compassion, kindness, humility, gentleness and patience; bearing with one another, and forgiving each other...just as the Lord forgave you, so also should you (Colossians 3:12-13).

Therefore, confess your sins to one another, and pray for one another so that you may be healed (James 5:16).

Therefore, laying aside falsehood, speak the truth each one of you with his neighbor, for we are members of one an-

other...Let no unwholesome word proceed from your mouth, but only such a word as is good for edification according to the need of the moment, so that it will give grace to those who hear...Let all bitterness and wrath and anger and clamor and slander be put away from you, along with all malice. Be kind to one another, tenderhearted, forgiving each other, just as God in Christ also has forgiven you (Ephesians 4:25, 29-32).

May we learn to walk in each of the Ways of God so we can experience the abundant life that Jesus promised!

Appendix VIII: NO FEAR IN LOVE

The English dictionary defines fear as: the feeling one has when danger, pain or trouble is near; the feeling of being worried or excited and wanting to run and hide.

A healthy concern and a hesitant caution are good things. These feelings are not fears although they can be precursors to fear. There are many things that cause us to fear. The things we tend to fear the most are:

• Harm—fearing something bad will happen to me

• Embarrassment—fearing I will be exposed for being or doing something others think is foolish

• Failure—fearing I will not be successful

• Loss—fearing I may lose what I have

• Future—fearing what will happen or not happen

• Unknown God—who may judge and condemn me

If fear is entertained for any sustained time, it can produce many ill side effects. Stress is one such side effect which can result in tunnel vision, loss of perception, and errors in judgment. Fear is also known to raise blood pressure and delete the immune system, inviting many physical and psychological maladies.

Old Testament Scriptures translate two very different Hebrew words as fear; *pachad* and *yare*. Both words are used to speak of a fear of the Lord. Let's compare them.

Pachad means "a dread." Pachad is a fearful dread that produces mistrust and fearfulness along with the accompanying side effects of anxiety, worry and stress.

And the dread [pachad—fear in KJV] *of God was on all the kingdoms of the lands when they heard that the Lord had fought against the enemies of Israel* (2 Chronicles 20:29).

These people had a good reason to fear God. If they fought Israel they could count on God being against them.

Yare, however means "reverence." Reverence produces feelings of love, honor, respect, trust, and gratitude.

The fear [yare-reverence] *of the LORD is the beginning of wisdom, and the knowledge of the Holy One is understanding* (Proverbs 9:10).

The secret of the LORD is for those who fear [yare-reverence] *Him, and He will make them know His covenant commitment* (Psalm 25:14).

The wise King Solomon wrote the book of Proverbs. He actually said the reverence of God is "the beginning of wisdom."

Most Bible translations translate yare as fear in each of the thirteen times it appears in Old Testament Scripture. Why? People were taught for centuries that we are to have a dreadful fear of God. Many conversions happened because God was presented as one to be feared.

Let's look at our beginnings. Our first parents, Adam and Eve's contact with God in the Garden of Eden did not produce any consciousness of fear or shame (see Genesis 2:25). Their reverent trust in God and each other produced only love and respect. When they traded God's guidance for a deception, it changed their perception. A dreadful fear replaced reverent trust. This distorted perception caused them to hide from God's presence.

> *They heard the sound of the Lord God walking in the Garden in the cool of the day, and the man and his wife hid themselves from the presence of the LORD God... Then the LORD God called to the man, and said to him, "Where are you?" And he said, "I heard the sound of You in the Garden, and I was afraid because I was naked; so I hid myself"* (Genesis 3:8-10).

God did not change, but outside of God's guiding fellowship, Adam and Eve did. They began to think of God as an adversary, feeling "He will hurt us." Dreadful fear clouded their ability to see God clearly, and they shrank from His coming presence.

The world has always recognized fear as a great motivator. Over the centuries many have used the fear of God and hellfire to keep people submissive. Terrorists are masters at using fear to subjugate people to their demands.

God, however, proclaimed through Jesus Christ that He forgives us and wants His love, not fear, to be our guiding influence. God's loving forgiveness demonstrates that He prefers us to respond out of a grateful heart rather than a fearful heart.

God is only Lord and Master of the willing, not of the fearful. Some of us may have come to God because of a fear of eternity, but we want to replace any such fear with a loving reverent trust of our heavenly Father.

Our release from an existing fear can come little by little, bit by bit, or in phenomenal leaps and bounds. The stronger our reverent trust and confidence in God becomes, the less we will fear all other factors.

Joseph's testimony captures the overriding effect that reverent trust in God can have on any ill that may come our way.

> *But Joseph said to them, "Do not be afraid, for am I in God's place? And as for you, you meant evil against me, but God meant it for good in order to bring about this present result"* (Genesis 50:19-20).

A mature, reverent trust in our heavenly Father will have a positive effect on how we respond to daily situations, to circumstances, to challenges, to trials, and to each other. A strong reverential trust and confidence in God is what keeps any of us from falling under fearful worry, stress, and anxiety.

Does fear have any hold on us? How fully do we trust God's ability to bring good out of our experiences? As offspring of God, we have a deep-seated need to rely on our heavenly Father as our protector and provider.

The following Scriptures can encourage our confident trust in God and help us turn away from fearfulness:

> *For He Himself has said, "I will never desert you, nor will I ever forsake you," so that we confidently say, "The Lord is my helper, I shall not be afraid. What shall man do to me?" ...Jesus Christ is the same yesterday and today, yes, and forever* (Hebrews 13:5-7).

> *When I am afraid, I will put my trust in Thee. In God, whose Word I praise, in God I have put my trust; I shall not be afraid. What can mere man do to me?* (Psalm 56:3-4)

I will bless the LORD at all times; His praise shall continually be in my mouth. My soul shall make its boast in the LORD; O magnify the LORD with me, and let us exalt His name together. I sought the LORD and He answered me, and delivered me from all my fears (Psalm 34:1-4).

And we know that God causes all things to work together for good to those who love God...What then shall we say to these things? If God is for us, who is against us? (Romans 8:28, 31).

"Thus says the LORD who made you and formed you from the womb, who will help you, 'Do not fear...Do not tremble and do not be afraid; have I not long since announced it to you and declared it? And you are my witnesses. Is there any God besides Me?'" (Isaiah 44:1-2, 8).

Keep sound wisdom and discretion...Then you will walk in your way securely, and your foot will not stumble. When you lie down, you will not be afraid; when you lie down your sleep will be sweet. Do not be afraid of sudden fear, nor the onslaught of the wicked when it comes; for the LORD will be your confidence (Proverbs 3:21, 23-26).

For God has not given us a spirit of fear, but of power and love and discipline (2 Timothy 1:7).

Do not be afraid, little flock, for your Father has chosen gladly to give you the Kingdom (Luke 12:32).

There is no fear in love; but perfect love casts out fear... and the one who fears is not perfected in love (1 John 4:18).

Such activity will increase and solidify in us a reverent trust in God. This kind of knowledge of the Holy One is understanding and the beginning of wisdom. As we allow God to govern, rule, and reign in our lives, we experience the kingdom of God.

Also read: Matthew 6:25-34 and Psalm 19:7-10, 14

For Additional Resources

Please visit:
http://relationalgospel.com
where you can find:

• A free, online presentation of
The Christ Culture, perfect for sharing with others.

• A downloadable *Leader's Resource Packet* for *The Christ Culture* (one-time $27 fee), which includes expanded group discussion questions (12 to 14 per chapter), before and after participant evaluation forms, and tips on how to bring out the best in your group participants, any or all of which can be freely copied for group use, and/or more intensive individual study. Purchase of the *Leader's Resource Packet* grants you unlimited copying of the included materials for your church or small group use.

• Information on purchasing printed copies of *The Christ Culture*, including substantial discounts on bulk quantities.

About the Author

Keith dedicated his life to our heavenly Father in his pre-teen years. During the teenage years, he became a strong student of the Scriptures. At 29 he married Nancy, and they have three children and four grandchildren.

Keith has ministered in a variety of Christian denominations, serving in many capacities including senior pastor.

For more than 20 years, Keith has helped authors with his warm, easygoing style in such publishing positions as Author/Editor Liaison, Director of Acquisitions, Assistant Publisher, and Literary Agent.

To contact Keith Carroll by email:
keith@RelationalGospel.com

or write to:
Keith Carroll
PO Box 428
Newburg, PA 17240